Go and Tell No One

Go and Tell No One

REMEMBER AND REST IN THE SECRET AND THE SACRED

Kristin Hill

ISBN: 1973946939
ISBN 13: 9781973946939
Library of Congress Control Number: 2017911770
CreateSpace Independent Publishing Platform
North Charleston, South Carolina

Introduction

Have you ever been asked the question, "what would you do all day if time or money wasn't a factor?" Or what about this one….? "What is one thing that you enjoy doing so much that you lose track of time or forget to eat?" I'll confess that for most of my life, I didn't really have an answer for that. Forget to eat? Ummm, nothing. (I'm like an infant and stick to a pretty strict 2-3 hour feeding schedule, no matter what the heck I'm doing.)

The only answer that has ever even rolled around the corners of my mind when pondering a question like that is…*antiquing*? And please know that when I say, "antiquing," what I really mean is not searching for *fine* antiques, but rather *treasure hunting in fields of long forgotten, discarded glorious junk.* To me, a perfect day would be strolling through miles of fields blooming with vintage antique treasures, right among the wildflowers and bluebonnets, in Round Top, Texas. My heartbeat quickens at the idea of pulling over, off the side of the road, to some dilapidated, hole-in-the-wall, with rows and rows of shelves piled high of worn, leather-bound books, and chippy furniture, and vintage finds, rich with the perfect patina. If the place doesn't smell like a mixture of your grandmother's house with notes of old book pages, a splash of mold and a touch of dust, well then…it just may be a little too fancy for me.

For as long as I can remember, I have just loved the *thrill of the hunt.* I love imagining who wrote an old postcard, or what mysterious lock a wrought iron skeleton key opened, once upon a time. Our home is filled with long forgotten, country church stained glass windows, chippy painted armoires and wooden dough bowls. We have two vintage steamer trunks that my husband rescued from a farmhouse in the North Georgia mountains, and I love to wonder where in the world they traveled before they came to live as coffee tables in our home. There is something so intrinsically beautiful and exhilarating to me about pouring slowly over items that look seemingly worn out, and discarded, and reimagining them in a new way. It is absolutely addicting to search for hidden gems in the most unlikely places and to find what was someone else's discarded trash, and turn it into our own little treasure. I guess it's partly the *treasure hunting* feel that is addicting…and maybe also, that whole concept of things being *redeemed and restored.* The way those concepts manifest may be different for each of us, but I really do think that God has set in our hearts, a longing for His redemption story, so it doesn't surprise me at all when that sort of thing stirs something deep in us.

I'll never forget when I realized that the "treasure hunting" excitement that I felt when I was antiquing, was really similar to the familiar feeling I got when I started studying the Bible *for myself.* As long as I can remember, I have loved and studied God's Word. I have always loved Bible Study. I have loved a lot of the same Bible Studies that you have probably loved too. God has broken into my world, pruned me, shaped me, lifted me, refined me, challenged me, encouraged me and called me closer in, through the study and teachings of wise ones who have gone before. My heart swells with gratitude for that.

I think in almost every season of my life, God in His kindness, has given me the gift of being able to sit shoulder to shoulder with friends, to learn, study and grow in His Word together. That is a gift that I don't take lightly, and one that has undoubtedly formed every bit of who I am. I have been shaped by the wisdom and amazing insight of some of the most beautiful Bible teachers, and I think that any moments spent in the pursuit of God's truth are moments, well-spent.

I will say this though…the first thirty or so years of the way I did Bible Study, I think I was simply soaking in the wisdom and teaching of those that had gone before. There is nothing more valuable than a firm foundation in God's Word, and learning from the wisdom of discerning teachers is certainly a gift. I've also learned though, that whoever was the first person to write this in a fortune cookie or on a doctor's office inspirational poster, was on to something:

> "Give a Man a Fish, and You Feed Him for a Day.
> Teach a Man to Fish, and You Feed Him for a Lifetime."

I wonder how often, we accidentally adopt the mindset that if we want fish, we need to go to the fisherman that have gone before us, to get them. In the same way, how many of us, even unknowingly, have developed a pattern of going to a book, or reading a blog, or listening to a sermon or a podcast, as the way to receive revelation and truth from God's Word? Learning from the wisdom of others is so important, and such a beautiful way to be challenged and inspired. But I wonder how often we miss the promptings of the Holy Spirit, and revelation from God's Word *to us individually*, when we get in the habit of waiting to be inspired and challenged by someone else, and *their* revelations from God's Word? There has probably never been a time in history that people have had easier access to all the wisdom of the ages. Today, we can easily hold in the palms of our hands (literally), the greatest teachings of the most brilliant theologians and Bible teachers of all time. And that is such a gift! The only problem comes when we get in the habit of letting that be *the only* way we encounter truth and wisdom from God's Word. It's like that analogy of the fish…it can be such a blessing when we are given a fish. It can be just what we need, right when we need it! But we need to remember that we've been equipped to fish for ourselves, anytime we want! We can't even imagine the blessing that awaits us!

In creating this Bible Study, my hope has been to remind you, and encourage you in *your own* pursuit of studying God's Word, for yourself! Several years ago, I started a journey of learning how to study my Bible with only paper, a pencil, my Bible and an open, prayerful, seeking heart. When I prayed those words in Psalm 119, "open my eyes to see wonderful things in Your Word," He more than answered. He drew me close and spoke into my heart, with His wisdom and encouragement that only God Himself could have known I needed, in the moment. The Jesus I came to know, spending day after day studying the beautiful words in the gospels, changed my heart forever. And it changed the way that I approach God's Word, as well.

The last several years, I have gathered women for Bible Study in that same way, and we have really learned together, how to position ourselves so that God opens our hearts and our eyes to understand His Word. It still surprises me a bit when a woman that has been walking with Jesus for a long time, realizes that she really hasn't been studying God's Word for herself, but instead, just waiting to receive and consume wisdom from God through other people, throughout her week. With access to so much truth and wisdom all around us, it's not surprising how often that happens. But in these last years, I have seen the most beautiful thing happen in my own heart, and in the hearts of so many women and girls that I love.

I have never felt a rush like the one I experience when God leads me on a journey of discovering truth in His Word, *for myself*! My new answer to that question we talked about at the beginning, is that I realize now, that I could definitely get lost in God's Word! Learning how to uncover the foundational truths tucked in the pages of My Bible, understanding how to interpret context and meaning from words translated from the sacred original Greek or Hebrew… It's treasure hunting for sure, and I love it!!! And what's even better is that Matthew 6:19 reminds us that the prize at the end of a treasure hunt in God's Word, is not one that moth and rust can destroy!

My greatest hope is that if you keep reading the pages of this Bible study, that you wouldn't just take my word for it. I promise that I'll offer you all the truth I have, but it would be the greatest compliment of my life if you'd read these words, close this book, and then open your Bible and go find out for yourself. God's Word is so full, that the treasure hunting will never end, and it just gets better, the deeper and deeper we go! Studying God's Word for ourselves, asking Him for wisdom and learning to hear His voice in our own lives, is like learning how to fish, and then having the ability to fish for a lifetime! With every fiber of my being, I believe that all Scripture is God-breathed…it is living and active and is able to teach us, correct us, encourage and train us. (1) And we don't have to wait for someone else to do that for us! He gives us everything we need to receive that from His Word, for ourselves.

I'm excited that we'll get to go on a journey and do some investigating together! There are so many hidden treasures tucked in the words of Jesus throughout the gospels, and in the "go and tell no one" passages we'll study together. We find so many of the other words of Jesus familiar when we read the gospels, that we often miss the diamond, wrapped in coal, just under the surface. Isn't it funny though, that sometimes the words we read right over the first time or two, are the ones that can take us to the highest heights and the deepest depths? When we take the time to look beyond the obvious and familiar things we see on the surface, and *really look*…sometimes that's where we find our greatest reward. Have you ever been on vacation, and instead of going to the popular places that everyone knows about, instead asked a local if there are any hidden, secret beaches or waterfalls or breathtaking views? Driving right past the crowds, and following the road less traveled, can so often lead us to the greatest experiences of our lives. That's how I've come to feel about these words of Jesus in the "go and tell no one" passages we're going to study together. They may not be the words that jump out to us at first, and we may not hear much about them, but when we uncover the truths from the heart of Jesus, just under the surface, we'll be sure to Remember and Rest in the Secret and the Sacred, like never before.

So, what do you think? Are you up for going treasure hunting together?

About This Study

Like most things, the message of "Go and Tell No One" is one of God's ancient truths, set in His Word, before time began, but only more recently set in my heart. He began this quiet work in my soul, that for a long season I assumed was just for my own heart, and for my own benefit. God used stories of Jesus to bring rest to the desperation I felt in wanting to follow Him, in a way that was right, and pleasing to Him. Getting to peek into the interactions of Jesus gave fresh clarity to some of the deepest longings of my heart. It is only out of obedience that I humbly offer my interpretation, through the lens of what God has shown and forever changed in me.

For the last year, I have tried *so hard* to get out of doing this study.

I kept telling the Lord, "You drew me close and opened my eyes to the beauty of the Secret and the Sacred, and You have reminded me over and over that *You* are the treasure, Jesus. What if a year of studying this every day was maybe *just for me*, and for the purpose of what You were stirring up in *my own heart*? Could we just leave it at that? The message is, after all, *go and tell no one*. That sounds good to me! How about, *I tell exactly no one*, but You can keep stirring it up in me…Ok, God?"

That is the prayer that kept rising out of my heart.
And you can see exactly where that got me.

Ultimately, the way Jesus broke open my heart and transformed me, and refined places hidden deep within me, has left me forever changed. This Bible Study came to be, not because I feel like an authority, and certainly not out of a desire to share my story, but because it feels like this is what God is stirring up in *all of us* right now…

I'm a regular girl. I've loved God and His Word for as long as I can remember, but I didn't go to seminary, and I'm not a seasoned theologian. I teach Bible Studies, but I'm not fluent in Hebrew or Greek. I love my Bible so much, but sometimes I wake up and start scrolling through Instagram before the thought ever occurs for me to open it. I so often forget what I already know to be true.

Here is what changed my heart forever. As I studied the gospels, the Jesus I got to know there *became so real to me*. I'll never forget a few years ago, the morning after I finished teaching through the gospel of John, I woke up *already missing Jesus* and longingly looking back at the time we'd spent. His words had become old, faithful friends that would preach to my own soul, each time I began to forget. I had that deep nostalgic feeling you get when you wake up at home, after a week away on the most glorious vacation. I had walked many miles together with Jesus on this journey and was forever marked by it.

In studying His Word, *for myself*, the Lord began crystallizing this thought I kept having. The Jesus I got to know in the gospels didn't spend His time only going to the holiest places and speaking with only the most devout, and righteous theologians. In fact, He did the exact opposite. He spent His days walking through towns, and on the boats of fishermen, and in the homes of kind companions. He didn't use crazy intimidating words or preach complex theological sermons. He sat at their tables, walked on their streets and He talked about things like bread and salt and light. He spoke in parables and He asked questions. He stepped into their everyday, ordinary lives, carrying His holiness right to them, with His new covenant. People kept expecting Him to take His place in the Temple, theorizing with the learned and the pious devout. But instead, He said things like, "let the little children come to Me." His followers called Him "Rabbi" and "Teacher," but He answered back, calling them "friends." After generations and lifetimes of people of faith being categorized by the amount of religious teaching they'd acquired, Jesus confused everyone when He called His disciples out from the most unacademic of places.

That has to mean something for us, right?

If Jesus Himself didn't limit His relationship to the religious professionals, wouldn't the truth in that carry over for us, too? I think the person of Jesus that I've come to know in the gospels, would want us to know and remember that we too, are His disciples, and that kitchen tables, and cubicles, and passenger seats, and park benches, are amazing places to see the Kingdom of God up close.

His Word is for *all* of us.
And *all* of His Word is for us.

That helps us remember that each one of us, can read, and study, and understand, and be transformed by His Word…and not just the familiar, felt-board, Sunday school lessons, and highlighted passages, but each and every word in it, familiar or not.

I think we'd probably all say that we are familiar with the "Go and Tell" passages in the Bible. We certainly hear often, how important is to share our faith, and most of us would probably champion the notion that the word of our testimony, is a way that God reveals Himself to a watching and listening world. How would we ourselves, even know the saving love of Jesus, if someone had not first told each of us?

When God began to open my eyes to the many times in Scripture that Jesus actually said, "*Go and Tell No One*," I had no idea just how much my heart would need to hear it. These words of Jesus began to change my thinking and my perception about what it could look like to follow Him, and share in the work of building His Kingdom. As I wrestled through these truths, I felt the Lord stirring up questions deep inside my own heart. What does it look like to really live a life, worthy of the calling of Jesus? Are others out there wrestling with these same questions… "am I doing this right?" or "does what I'm doing even matter?" How many of us cry out with the prayers of our heart saying, "Jesus, I want to know you and make you known, for your glory and the good of others… I want to be an image bearer that walks with both humility and boldness, but what does that even look like, in today's world?"

In sitting with all this, and learning and studying, I just felt the Lord affirming that this is *His Word, His Truth*, and there are so many things that we, as believers of Jesus living in our world today, need to unlearn and relearn. And sometimes we need to remember what we already know to be true. With those very stirrings, deep in our hearts, in 2010, my husband Eric and I began "Withyou Ministries." We create resources and experiences to help people rest and remember that God is *withyou*. For years, God has allowed us to see up close, what it looks like for a soul to find its rest, in Christ alone. Of course, it's an ongoing, transforming work that is continuing always in our own hearts, but it's the part of the story that led me here. It is the joy of our lives to walk alongside people that the Lord brings our way. It is such a privilege to listen on their behalf, to remind them of what they already know is true…who Jesus already is, and who He says that we already are in Him… and to *remember and rest in the already-ness* of what He's done for us, and how the truth of that invites us into true freedom.

I'll never forget a few years ago, we had a particularly significant Withyou meeting with someone we'd come to love dearly. That person had shared longings and cried tears from the deepest depths, quietly, right there at our kitchen table, and then began again, to remember and rest in Jesus. It occurred to me that day, that most of my favorite memories in ministry, have been moments that *we'll never speak of again*. No one will ever know. They are too intimate…too sacred, and very often, not even our story to tell. Even with that new realization, it wasn't long before I felt the ongoing tension that would somehow rise up. How do you tell the story of God…how do you preach to your own soul first, and then encourage those beside you, when some moments are too secret and too sacred to share?

On our covered porch, on a beautiful summer morning several months later, I sat with my Bible open, and in that honest place in my soul where I can share the good, and the bad, and the ugly with Jesus. I have come to love the words of the Psalmist, "Search me and know me, God. Try my anxious heart, and see if there is any hurtful way, and lead me in the way everlasting." I have learned to welcome His sifting…to trust how He leads with the Light of His Word…how He shines His revealing light on anything untrue…even if just the slightest bit, and replaces it with His Truth. That morning on the porch, I sat in the tension that is so often a reality for believers of Jesus, in this day and age. At any moment in time, I can glance down at my phone and in just a minute or two of scrolling, see the countless, creative and significant ways, that other followers of Jesus are doing amazing things for Him, and I begin to wonder about the way I'm following Jesus with my own life. Does that resonate, at all, withyou too? That day, in that place of total honesty, and in the tenderness of that moment, the Holy Spirit brought to my remembrance, something I'd read before in God's Word. I spent a few minutes searching, and sure enough, there they were…the words of Jesus: "*Go and tell no one.*" Time after time, I continued to see in Scripture that Jesus had the most amazing, life-changing encounters with people and then he would literally say, "*…now, go and tell no one.*"

It may seem strange at first, but it doesn't take long to remember the upside-down way of Jesus, and how the gospels tell us over and over, about how He is after our hearts. He says those words for a reason, and *not just a few times, either*. So, it would do our hearts some good to see what these particular words are all about. Like I mentioned before, there is not much that I love more than a treasure hunt…whether it's looking for hidden treasures in a Texas field of junky antiques, or looking for hidden treasures in God's Word! The hunt is always worth it, and at least in the case of God's Word, it never ever returns void. The journey in trying to understand those words of Jesus, *"go and tell no one…"* has been one of the sweetest journeys of my life. The deeper I looked, the more His Words began to reveal, and the more I wanted the spirit of those words to ring true. It's a conversation that I believe to be timely for us, as we long to follow Jesus in a world that is constantly begging for our affections. The Jesus I see in these stories is even more tender, and more intentional than I knew, and the way He anticipates the tension in my heart, makes me feel known and understood. These truths in His Word have forever changed me, and they have given me new eyes to see, what a life following Jesus can really look like.

Jesus, *You are the treasure*. Teach our hearts what is true.
Help us to Remember and Rest in the Secret and the Sacred, withyou…

A Prayer Before We Begin...

So, we're about to take the first step on our journey together, and I want to make sure you have the road map. You won't hear much more about me or the journey God has taken me on specifically, but you will see the path opening up before us, as we walk these steps in tandem. During our six weeks together, we'll read and study, while each day, God stirs up truth in our hearts and seals it deep within our souls. The words of Jesus are so *beautifully crucial* to our lives... we need them like the very air we breathe, and we'll want to honor Jesus by seeking to understand His words with as much diligence and clarity as possible. We'll get to peek in and marvel as the inerrant, living and breathing truth in God's Word *builds the case for Itself.* If we imagine a painting coming to life on a blank canvas before us, then the first time we read a passage will create the first traces of the charcoal outline of what is to come. We'll see then, how *the same passage in other gospels*, give depth and color and bring out light and shadows we hadn't seen before. Glimpses into the *original language* will give precise details to the full picture, allowing us to see the masterpiece as a whole. For this work of art, the only medium used, will be God's Word itself, and we'll watch as it builds, and layers, and reveals things we didn't even know were there. And then, once the painting is set in its glory before us, we'll get to step back and take plenty of time to reflect on *what God is stirring up inside of us.* As we try to take it in, we'll often feel *the invitation* in the quiet, tender words from Jesus, and also *the challenge* in hearing His voice, amidst the clanging noise around us. Each time we approach His Word, we'll be met with an opportunity to see and uncover subtleties we hadn't maybe seen before, and the choice will be ours to let *His truth transform us.* And finally, the journey each week will lead us on a path through days that prompt us to first *Remember and then Rest, in the Secret and the Sacred.*

This is not quick and systematic work. It is not a mindless checking off of boxes. Just as breathtaking art needs the luxury of time and space to be created, this process too will require time and space in order to become exactly what it's supposed to be. The very process of letting God's Word transform us, mirrors the meandering, progressing creation of art, itself. *It's ok for it to go slowly.* Isn't that the way it is with all the best things in life?

So, here are my prayers for us as we begin...

I pray that we'll *savor the journey.* I pray that we'll feel permission to courageously dip below the way things appear on the surface, and pay attention to what Christ is stirring deep within us. I pray we'll wrestle, and do the hard work of coming to understand, even the unfamiliar words of Jesus. I pray we will come to love Him in ways, our hearts have never known, and I pray that we'll emerge on the other side, transformed by Him forever.

And the greatest prayer of my heart is that these words of Jesus— *"Go and Tell No One,"* — *will lead us to forever, Remember and Rest in the Secret and Sacred.*

Week 1

Day 1

No matter how we feel when we open our Bibles to study Scripture, we can trust God's Word to be alive, and active, with the power to move, refine, and transform us. We can also rest assured that the Holy Spirit is moving in ways we cannot see, to open our hearts and minds, and to stir up Christ in us. So often, we approach God's Word with a "quick fix" mentality, in hopes of getting ourselves back on track, making life work, even if just on the surface. My hope for us, instead, is that we would approach God's Word in a new way… allowing it to soak into the deep and unseen places of our hearts, that hold feelings and longings and emotions that are not often or easily articulated. Let's position ourselves to read God's Word in a way that stirs up what is best in us…Christ, the hope of glory.

I wish I was more of a gardener. I am betting though, that even the most unskilled among us, have at least *a loose* understanding of how things grow. If there is a tree in my yard, and I notice that it has dead leaves, I can easily understand that simply pulling off the dead leaves, won't prevent the tree from ever having dead leaves again. It is important to look at the roots, and how they are being nourished, and what other factors are affecting the health of the tree from the inside out, especially in the unseen places where the roots live. Only then can I understand what is truly going on inside the tree. The way the leaves look on the surface is just a picture of what is going on deep inside. Simply treating the leaves themselves, without ever looking at the roots, would be simply treating the symptoms. Nothing will change in the tree, until what is going on inside the tree is considered, as well. It is the same with God's Word and the work of the Holy Spirit in our lives. Deep soul-stirring transformation is ours in Christ if we are willing to let His Word do its deep, refining work within us…. even, at the root of the root.

As we read God's Word together and look closely at the words of Jesus, let's look first at what is going on at the surface. And then, let's fix our eyes beyond that, to look at what is going on deep inside, as well.

Let's begin to read God's Word, to study it inductively, understanding context and meaning, but also with the purpose, and from the posture of allowing God to stir up things deep within us. Any time spent studying God's word, and getting to know the heart of Jesus, is time well spent. Praying that today He opens our eyes to the wonders in His Word!

Open your Bible and let's read this passage together, in Matthew 8:1-4.

Matthew 8:1-4 (NASB)
When Jesus came down from the mountain, large crowds followed Him.
2 And a leper came to Him and bowed down before Him, and said,
"Lord, if You are willing, You can make me clean." 3 Jesus stretched
out His hand and touched him, saying, "I am willing; be cleansed."
And immediately his leprosy was cleansed. 4 And Jesus said to him,
"See that you tell no one; but go, show yourself to the priest and pres-
ent the offering that Moses commanded, as a testimony to them."

If you can, read this short text several times today, meditating on the passage, and recording observations. Continue to pray and ask God what treasures are tucked away in this passage, and end by asking yourself these questions:

What does this mean?

Why does it matter?

What is Christ stirring up in me when I read this?

Day 2

Yesterday we took the first few steps on our journey together. We read the first of several passages, where we see Jesus having a truly life-changing encounter with someone, and then giving instructions for that person not to tell anyone else about it. I know the Lord will continue to stir up so much in our own hearts, but before we jump in any further, in order to make sure we understand and interpret this passage correctly, let's make sure we know as much as we can about the context.

Let's look at Matthew 8:1-4 again, and answer the "WH questions," described in the Appendix: Bible Study Methods, to get a good idea of what exactly is going on here.

Who is talking, and to whom are they speaking?

What is happening in this text? What happened just before?

When did this interaction take place? (Answer both, in chronological terms, as well as in the context of what was happening in the life and ministry of Jesus. You can look at what was happening in the passages and chapters before this one, if that helps.)

<u>Why</u> is this interaction important?

<u>Where</u> did this happen, and was the location important? Were other people in this same place and able to hear this conversation?

<u>How</u> does this interaction apply to me?

Is there anything else significant that jumps out at me right away? What can I learn about Jesus? What is Christ stirring up in me as I read this?

This passage may have felt familiar, for the most part…until we get to the words of Jesus in verse 4. We see that Jesus shows great compassion, and He heals the man of his leprosy—instantly, in fact. Scripture is full of stories about the power of Jesus bringing physical healing. The beauty and complexities of those stories and the topic of healing are worthy of their own study, for sure. For our purposes here, we want to look less at what is happening visibly, and more at what is happening underneath the surface, in the hearts of both Jesus, and the person He heals. With that in mind, read the passage again, and write down the first command that Jesus gave after healing the man's leprosy?

So, what in the world is that about? Any ideas why Jesus would say that?

Jesus gave that first command largely because of what was going on in the larger story, and He gave a second command based on what was going on in this particular man's life, within the context of the larger story. The issue here was not one of obedience to Jesus, but rather of obedience to the Old Testament Law still in place, as given in Leviticus 14. If a leper believed himself healed, he must show himself to the priest and if indeed, the leprosy was gone, there were certain cleansing rituals and sacrifices that must be made before he was allowed to return to his community. Knowing that helps us to understand Jesus' second command, for the man to go show himself to the priest. But what about that first command? "See that you tell no one." We don't have to do much research or study, to imagine that Jesus healing a leper, fully *in an instant*, would be no small miracle! The text says, "immediately his leprosy was cleansed!" Can you even imagine witnessing that? And then, instead of basking in the moment, Jesus seems to not want the credit, and He even seems to take steps to prevent getting any attention or praise from the interaction. Write down your observations about Jesus in this passage:

Let's look at the same passage, through the lens of a different translation. Matthew 8:1-4, in the Message, says this:

Matthew 8:1-4 (MSG)
1-2 Jesus came down the mountain with the cheers of the crowd still ringing in His ears. Then a leper appeared and went to his knees before Jesus, praying, "Master, if you want to, you can heal my body."
3-4 Jesus reached out and touched him, saying, "I want to. Be clean." Then and there, all signs of the leprosy were gone. Jesus said, "Don't talk about this all over town. Just quietly present your healed body to the priest, along with the appropriate expressions of thanks to God. Your cleansed and grateful life, not your words, will bear witness to what I have done."

Did reading this translation spark any new thoughts about why this interaction may be significant? If so, write them down here...

Day 3

We've spent the last 2 days looking at a story out of the gospel of Matthew. As is so often the case, one or both of the other Synoptic gospels, tells the same story, giving a few, added details. And if that is an unfamiliar term, "synoptic gospels" simply refers to the gospels of Matthew, Mark, and Luke. They are referred to in this way because they include many of the same stories, often in the same sequence, and with similar wording. It's as if all three books are giving us a similar, but not identical, synopsis of an interaction. The beautiful gospel of John, by the way, is equally important. John's content and format are simply presented differently.

Let's look at this same story we read about on Day 1 and Day 2, but as it's presented in **Mark 1:40-45**, as well as in **Luke 5:12-16.**

Mark 1:40-45 (NASB)
40 And a leper came to Jesus, beseeching Him and falling on his knees before Him, and saying, "If You are willing, You can make me clean." 41 Moved with compassion, Jesus stretched out His hand and touched him, and said to him, "I am willing; be cleansed." 42 Immediately the leprosy left him and he was cleansed. 43 And He sternly warned him and immediately sent him away, 44 and He said to him, "See that you say nothing to anyone; but go, show your- self to the priest and offer for your cleansing what Moses com- manded, as a testimony to them." 45 But he went out and began to proclaim it freely and to spread the news around, to such an extent that Jesus could no longer publicly enter a city, but stayed out in un- populated areas; and they were coming to Him from everywhere."

So, this telling gives us a bit more information. On your own, read the account in **Luke 5:12-16** as well, and piece together what seemed to have happened afterward, as a result. With this in mind, do you have any new insights about why, after Jesus healed the leper, He commanded the man not to tell anyone what happened?

Scripture tells us of many interactions of Jesus that are similar to His encounter with the leper in Matthew 8. Today we will dive into another encounter that happens, soon after, in Matthew 9.

Read Matthew 9:27-31

Matthew 9:27-31 (ESV)

27 And as Jesus passed on from there, two blind men followed him, crying aloud, "Have mercy on us, Son of David." 28 When He entered the house, the blind men came to Him, and Jesus said to them, "Do you believe that I am able to do this?" They said to him, "Yes, Lord." 29 Then He touched their eyes, saying, "According to your faith be it done to you." 30 And their eyes were opened. And Jesus sternly warned them, "See that no one knows about it." 31 But they went away and spread his fame through all that district.

In the interest of being thorough, and to practice using God's Word to illuminate God's Word, read the same passage in the Message translation:

Matthew 9:27-31 (MSG)

27-28 As Jesus left the house, he was followed by two blind men crying out, "Mercy, Son of David! Mercy on us!" When Jesus got home, the blind men went in with Him. Jesus said to them, "Do you really believe I can do this?" They said, "Why, yes, Master!" 29-31 He touched their eyes and said, "Become what you believe." It happened. They saw. Then Jesus became very stern. "Don't let a soul know how this happened." But they were hardly out the door before they started blabbing it to everyone they met.

Using your favorite inductive Study Method, write out your observations.

(Don't peek at any commentaries just yet!)

What is similar to the interaction we studied earlier this week?

What is different?

Day 4

You may already be forming some ideas about why we continue to see Jesus giving this unfamiliar command to "go and tell no one." Let's continue searching these Scriptures, seeking to understand the context and reasons behind these words of Jesus. Read **Matthew 9:27-31** again.

How do the two blind men address Jesus? Do you recall any other parts of Scripture where that term is used? And if so, what does that imply?

The name by which these two blind men addressed Jesus was "Son of David." When we study the occurrences of that title being used for Jesus within the gospels, we find that it is almost always used by crowds or by people who knew Jesus only at a distance. The term "Son of David" describes Jesus in the popular conception of the Messiah, rather than the personal. For centuries, the Jewish people had awaited the promised deliverer of David's line. They anxiously looked for the leader who would not only restore their freedom but who would lead them to power and glory and greatness. Most of the nation was looking for a Messiah who would be a political revolutionary. They were looking for a king who would come in and release the nation from Roman domination. Many people saw the supernatural power of Jesus and were drawn to what His power could do for them personally, as well as politically. It was in that way that these blind men thought of Jesus; they saw in Him the wonder-worker who would lead the people to freedom and to conquest. They came to Jesus with a very incomplete and inadequate idea of who and what He was, and yet He healed them. (1) The way in which Jesus interacted with them is fascinating.

There is a progression from when the two blind men first cry out to Jesus, and then when their personal interaction with Him occurred. What do you notice about the setting, and about that progression?

Clearly, Jesus did not answer the men when they first called out to Him, as He passed. It is interesting to note that Jesus, instead began to interact with the men, only after they were away from the crowds on the street. And once behind closed doors, Jesus asked them a question that would reveal the true posture of their hearts towards Him. Why do you think that is?

In Matthew 9: 30, it says that "Jesus sternly warned them, saying, "See here, let no one know about this!" Did they follow His command, and what are your thoughts on that?

With the earthly ministry of Jesus set in motion, the plan for the greatest redemption story of all time had come to earth. Jesus, Himself came and turned everything that had ever been known, upside down and inside out. It was no surprise to Jesus, the way that people would react to Him, after getting a glimpse of the divinity that was intertwined with His humanity. It was important for people to see the person of Jesus…to hear His teaching, and His gospel of grace and truth and freedom. His words, His life, and His message were unlike anything the world had ever seen. It has been proven over and over again, that God knows the hearts of His people, and He knew the tendency for people to skip over the transformational gospel of good news, and fixate instead, on the shock and awe of His power, and His ability to heal and perform supernatural miracles. The heart of Jesus for His people was not *just* to meet their physical needs, and bring healing to their bodies, but also to bring healing, freedom to their souls, and reconciliation with God for eternity. Jesus knew that without the context of His message, and His teaching, that many would come to Him only interested in a simple transaction, for how He could meet their needs. *Jesus knew the tendency of people to focus on the miraculous more than the Message, and on the gifts more than the Giver.*

There were certainly specific circumstances at the time, that caused Jesus to want to keep many interactions with people a secret. The heart of man, however, is a common thread weaving throughout generation to generation. Can you relate to the concept that a person could approach God, without fully understanding who He is, and with a desire simply for his or her individual needs to be met? How often does the heart of Jesus compel us to follow Him, further up and further in, so that we are positioned better to receive more fully, His truth, grace, freedom, and blessing? How often do we forfeit a personal, and sacred encounter with Jesus, because we settle for a more general, corporate approach to Him, where little is required of us individually? Think about how often we may approach God in these ways, and what He may think about that. Do you ever find yourself approaching God, asking Him to be something He is not? Write your thoughts here…

Day 5

So far, this week, we have looked at a few passages where we see Jesus having a life-changing interaction with someone, and then giving them strict instructions to tell no one about it. Even though "Messiah" is the most frequently used title for Jesus by the New Testament authors, it was not a title that Jesus used very often for Himself. Jesus' guarding of His identity for much of His earthly ministry is typically referred to as the "Messianic Secret." (2.) At the time, most of the nation failed to grasp the full role of the Messiah, especially those foretold in the prophetic writings, such as Isaiah 53. Those Old Testament Scriptures revealed that the Messiah would not simply be a political ruler, but also a suffering servant. We see in the gospels, that many times Jesus sought to keep His divine identity hidden if it was not introduced within the context of His preaching.

Scripture paints a picture for us, of the three in one Trinity. The Father, Son, and Holy Spirit who collectively orchestrated a plan to rescue, redeem, and restore all mankind…sinful people, passionately loved by God, yet separated from Him. In His perfect omniscience, God knew the nature of humanity, and how each generation often finds themselves misunderstanding the ways of God. The humans walking the earth, during the actual time of Jesus, were no different. God's people were desperate for a king, a leader, and someone who could sweep in with power and save them. Jesus had absolutely come in power, but His rescue plan would look nothing like they had expected. The perfect Messiah intimately knew the hearts of these people, and He knew that they would need to hear Him teach the gospel if they were ever going to understand the upside-down ways of the Kingdom, for themselves. In each of the passages that we read, Jesus was reaching out with compassion, power, humility, and with the heart of both the Messiah, as well as a teacher, and healer. In compassion, He brought exactly what was needed…supernatural physical healing, divine wisdom, and revelation, and the invitation for a personal encounter with the Messiah. In every interaction, the trajectories of each of these lives would forever be changed. The Greek word "kairos," is a fitting term that describes an appointed season, or an opportune time, and we often think about it in terms of God breaking into our everyday lives. It seems that the people encountering Jesus in the passages we read this week would likely measure their lives by the context, "before I understood who Jesus was," and "after." There was an invitation in each of these encounters, but it was personal, and not meant to be for the masses. There would be an appointed time, that all would be revealed, and all would know that Jesus, was in fact, who He said He was… but it was not yet that time. Jesus still had teaching to do…it was still a season of preparation. Jesus knew that if the "shock and awe" of who He really was spread too quickly, and without the foundation of His teaching, that the people would completely miss the root of the gospel. He foreknew the depths of the heart of His people, and He knew that there would be a tendency to focus on the miracles performed, and the related outcomes, rather than the message He proclaimed. It was the season for quiet, small encounters with the Messiah…for true understanding to come through teaching, and personal interactions. It was a season for hearing the voice of Jesus, to learn His wisdom, and truth about the Kingdom of God. It was organic and grassroots, and it was meant to be personal…life-giving and life-changing. Jesus knew that one day, the story of His life, and the way that He came to us, would be known by *all*…but it wasn't yet time to turn to that part of the story.

When we read specific stories in God's Word, about encounters that Jesus had with people, we are given an invitation to learn more about Jesus, as well as ourselves, by what He stirs up in us. At the very root of good, inductive, personal Bible Study is a respectful and thorough look at the context, meaning, and purpose of a passage. Then, with greater understanding, we are able to look for the promptings of the Holy Spirit to help us recognize and identify where God is stirring our hearts, and already at work in our own lives today.

Let's close today, by taking a prayerful look back over the passages we've read this week. *Choose one passage specifically*, and answer these questions.

1.   What did this Scripture mean when it was written?

2.   What is the timeless truth behind what God is saying?

3.   How does it apply to me now?

We understand that the heart of Jesus is that we would come to know Him and understand Him, within the context of who He really is. Scripture often describes "the mystery of Christ," and while our earthly minds will never know the *full* depths of all that there is to know about Him, there is a difference between knowing Him, and His mystery, *in part*, and having an *inaccurate* or *inadequate* picture of who He truly is. In your own words, and from your own journey to knowing Christ through His Word, answer this question. Who is Jesus to me?

Day 6/ Remember

Throughout Scripture, we see that the way of Jesus, when He interacts with people, is to ask questions to reveal the true, deep-down condition of their hearts. We want to use Days 6, and 7, each week to pay attention to all that Jesus may be stirring up in us, and to hold God's Word up as a mirror to show and reflect what we may not be able to clearly see, on our own.

We also want to use these days to help us to build in rhythms of time and space, to remember what we already know to be true and to find rest in the words of Jesus. We need to preach back to our own souls, what God says about Himself, and what He says about us. We need to quiet the noise of the world, and the swirling thoughts and emotions we feel, and anchor our souls to God's Word, and *remember and rest.*

In the passages we read this week, we saw several instances of a person having a life-changing, life-altering encounter with Jesus, only then to receive instructions from Him, to keep it quiet. Everything we've read reminds us about the upside-down ways of Jesus. He came in a way that no one suspected, He spoke words that were the opposite of what everyone else was saying. He taught that the first shall be last, and the last shall be first. He interacted with the outcast that everyone else set aside. He carried healing in His hands and could change a life with a single touch, but often seemed to want none of the credit or attention. And when it seemed like it would make sense, to spread the good news of what He had done, Jesus instead gave instructions not to tell anyone what had happened.

In John 14:26, Jesus describes the role of the Holy Spirit in our lives. He says, "the Helper, the Holy Spirit, whom the Father will send in My name, He will teach you all things, and bring to your remembrance all that I said to you." After studying the passages we've read this week, what has He taught you or brought to your remembrance again, about Jesus?

In the passages we studied this week, we saw that the heart of Jesus was for people to understand who He was, in the context of the gospel that He not only preached but lived, as well. He seemed to know the tendency for people to begin to view Him with an inadequate picture of who He was, and what He came to do. Do you think that happens today, and if so, how can we remember who Jesus really is?

Another thing we saw Jesus frequently doing, was drawing a person away from the crowd, and into a more intimate, often secret, encounter. It would seem that sometimes the treasure of knowing and following Jesus is found in the Secret and the Sacred, not in the public or the visible. Why do you think we continue to see Jesus drawing people away from the crowd, into the Secret, and what might that look like in our own sacred relationship with Him today?

What do you think it would be like to have such a life-altering encounter with Jesus, but then to have Him instruct you not to tell anyone about it? Have you ever felt Him asking you to do something you didn't understand or didn't seem to make sense?

These passages remind us that God is always reaching in, and working in "the kairos moments" of our own lives. We remember also, that our own individual stories sit within the larger story He is writing. Is it possible that sometimes Jesus asks us to obey, even if it doesn't make sense to us, because of what He is doing in the larger story? Write your thoughts here.

Lord, even though we are just beginning, after reading and studying this week, I *remember again* who You are.

What I most feel you stirring up in me is…

Day 7/ Rest

Lord, when I think about Your heart, and I remember that above all else, You are after my heart, I am prompted to position myself to truly encounter who You are.

Lord, is it possible that there are times that I have been like the people in the passages this week? Have I, in the past, had an inaccurate or inadequate picture of who You are? Do I have the tendency to approach You because of what You can do for me, instead of approaching You with a desire to worship and know You?

In the passage this week, I saw Jesus drawing the blind men away from the crowd, and into an intimate experience with Him alone. In fact, for both the leper and the blind men, it was the encounters with Jesus, in private, away from the crowds, that were life-changing.

Lord, I know your heart is not just for me to be withyou only in the large group settings that may be a part of my week. But also, I know Your desire for me, is to be withyou in secret and sacred encounters alone, as well. This is what I feel you stirring in me...

Jesus, I remember again that even when people didn't understand fully who you were, or understand what you were doing in the larger story, you remained unchanged. When I stop and remember, I can rest in who you are, and what you have already done.

This week I have learned to remember...

And, when I remember, I can rest...

Jesus, in light of what I have learned this week, and as I position my heart to remember and rest, this is my prayer....

Week 2

Day 1

On our journey this week, we are going to ask the Lord to open our minds to understand the Scriptures, by continuing to use Bible Study methods that bring clarity and revelation. And as we do, we'll both study for ourselves, and pay attention to what Christ is stirring in us, as we encounter Him in our own secret and sacred places.

We are living in a day and age, where we have easy and immediate access to some of the greatest Bible teachers of our time. It can be easy to simply listen and consume the wisdom and revelation of others, without ever doing the work of letting God's Word teach, transform, correct, and train our hearts, first *for ourselves, individually*.

One of my deepest prayers for this study is that you would grow in the confidence that in studying God's Word, you already have everything you need, in Christ. It is always a blessing to learn from the wisdom of those who have gone before us, but if we are not careful, we can become lazy in our personal pursuit of God, if all we ever do is take other peoples' word for it. The Bible is living and active, and God uses it to draw us back to His heart, and to speak to us individually! Scripture is full of treasures, and sometimes we just need reminding that we already have the tools that can lead us to the treasure.

When we think about the interactions that Jesus had, we are reminded yet again, that *His gospel is for everyone*. We remember again, that Jesus didn't spend time only with the learned, prestigious theologians, but instead, He walked with everyday, ordinary people, on the streets of their towns, and on the shores of the sea. He spent His time talking with fisherman, and carpenters, and mothers, and fathers and children. He didn't use big, complex words that no one could understand...He spoke about the Kingdom of God, using objects like salt, and water, and bread, and seeds, and light. He often spoke in parables, telling stories that would paint a picture of the Kingdom truths He was teaching about. But even in His parables, He required that the listeners be *active participants*, in hearing the stories, and then thinking about what they meant, in real life.

If Jesus were here and walking the earth among us today, I think He'd maybe want us to remember, that His Word is not only *approachable*, but it is *available* to *each* of us right now, and able to speak into the deepest parts of our hearts. We can certainly learn and gain wisdom from pastors, and teachers, and sermons and podcasts, and Bible Studies. But we can also open our Bibles right where we are today, and let His Word speak into our hearts. Anytime we seek to understand a passage in its fullness, by inductively studying its context, setting, content, meaning and intent, we are already studying, for ourselves. When we are seeking to honor, understand, explain and rightly interpret a passage in Scripture, even if we weren't calling it by its name, we've already taken part in, what is called "exegesis." When our heart's desire is to fully understand God's Word, whether by simply looking to see what the words meant in the original language, or whether we are using specific methods to help us gain clarity about a passage, we invite God to bring His truth to our own hearts, and stir our souls. A favorite scholar, pastor, and teacher that I have learned so much from talks about studying God's Word this way:

"Too many Bible readers assume that exegesis is what you do after you have learned Greek and Hebrew. That's simply not true. Exegesis is nothing more than a careful and loving reading of the text in our mother tongue. Greek and Hebrew are well worth learning, but if you haven't had the privilege, settle for English. Once we learn to love this text and bring a disciplined intelligence to it, we won't be far behind the very best Greek and Hebrew scholars. Appreciate the learned Scripture scholars, but don't be intimidated by them. Exegesis is the furthest thing from pedantry; exegesis is an act of love. *It loves the one who speaks the words enough to want to get the words right.* It respects the words enough to use every means we have to get the words right. Exegesis is loving God enough to stop and listen carefully to what He says....

Exegesis does not mean mastering the text, it means submitting to it as it is given to us. Exegesis doesn't take charge of the text and impose superior knowledge on it; it enters the world of the text and *lets the text 'read' us. Exegesis is an act of sustained humility.*" (1)

To set the tone for our study this week, let's read this passage together:

2 Timothy 3:16-17
16 "All Scripture is God-breathed and is useful for teaching, rebuking, correcting and training in righteousness, 17 so that the servant of God may be thoroughly equipped for every good work."

It can take great courage to read God's Word and begin to interpret what His words mean. That is true enough with the passages that are straightforward, and familiar to us, much less the unfamiliar ones! The words of Jesus in the "go and tell no one" passages, may not feel familiar or obvious at first, but we love Him enough to want to get His words right. In the spirit of 2nd Timothy, we believe those Words of Jesus to be just as God-breathed and useful to us, and our faith, as the more familiar ones. Write out what you are feeling as we continue on this journey together...

Day 2

Today we are going to jump in and continue reading and studying the words of Jesus, as they lead us to Remember and Rest in the Secret and the Sacred.

Let's begin by reading Mark 3: 7-12.

Mark 3:7-12 (NASB)

7 Jesus withdrew to the sea with His disciples; and a great multitude from Galilee followed; and also from Judea, 8 and from Jerusalem, and from Idumea, and beyond the Jordan, and the vicinity of Tyre and Sidon, a great number of people heard of all that He was doing and came to Him. 9 And He told His disciples that a boat should stand ready for Him because of the crowd, so that they would not crowd Him; 10 for He had healed many, with the result that all those who had afflictions pressed around Him in order to touch Him. 11 Whenever the unclean spirits saw Him, they would fall down before Him and shout, "You are the Son of God!" 12 And He earnestly warned them not to tell who He was.

And now, let's look at that scene again, through the lens of a different translation.

Mark 3:7-12 The Message (MSG)

7-10 Jesus went off with His disciples to the sea to get away. But a huge crowd from Galilee trailed after them—also from Judea, Jerusalem, Idumea, across the Jordan, and around Tyre and Sidon—swarms of people who had heard the reports and had come to see for themselves. He told his disciples to get a boat ready so He wouldn't be trampled by the crowd. He had healed many people, and now everyone who had something wrong was pushing and shoving to get near and touch Him. 11-12 Evil spirits, when they recognized Him, fell down and cried out, "You are the Son of God!" But Jesus would have none of it. He shut them up, forbidding them to identify Him in public.

Let's try using the same "WH question" progression that we used in week one:

<u>Who</u> is talking, and to whom are they speaking?

<u>What</u> is happening in this text? What happened just before?

<u>When</u> did this interaction take place? (Answer both, in chronological terms, as well as in the context of what was happening in the life and ministry of Jesus. Feel free to look at what was happening in the passages and chapters before this one.)

<u>Why</u> is this interaction important?

<u>Where</u> did this happen, and was the location important?

How does this interaction apply to us, today?

We have now read several accounts where Jesus gives strict instructions to those He encountered, not tell anyone.

Is there a common thread throughout these interactions?

We are getting to look at what it was like in the local areas, as Jesus' ministry began unfolding, and news of Him began to spread. What are your impressions, and what is God stirring up in you, as you reflect on what you have read and studied?

Day 3

Yesterday we read a passage from Mark 3. Today we are going to pick up with a passage just a few chapters later in Mark 7.

Read Mark 7:31-37 (NIV)
31 "Then Jesus left the vicinity of Tyre and went through Sidon, down to the Sea of Galilee and into the region of the Decapolis. 32 There some people brought to him a man who was deaf and could hardly talk, and they begged Jesus to place His hand on him. 33 After He took him aside, away from the crowd, Jesus put his fingers into the man's ears. Then He spit and touched the man's tongue. 34 He looked up to heaven and with a deep sigh said to him, "Ephphatha!" (which means "Be opened!"). 35 At this, the man's ears were opened, his tongue was loosened and he began to speak plainly. 36 Jesus commanded them not to tell anyone. But the more He did so, the more they kept talking about it. 37 People were overwhelmed with amazement. "He has done everything well," they said. "He even makes the deaf hear and the mute speak."

Using whatever inductive study method you'd like, record your major impressions, and observations. (Refer to the Appendix, if you want to try a new method.)

What do you think are the most significant portions of this text, and why? What is the application for those in the passage? How might that apply to you, today?

In verse 33 yet again, we see an encounter where Jesus hears the cry of a soul in need and attends to that person's need, but only after "taking that person aside, away from the crowd." What are your thoughts, as you read that?

In verse 36, we see the familiar command from Jesus not to tell anyone. Why do you think Jesus continues to give this command?

It is important to reinforce, again, that much of the reason that Jesus gave this command in the interactions we have read about is, that Jesus did not want the news of Him being the Messiah to spread too quickly and without context, and without the foundation of His teaching.

Didn't Jesus know that stories of miracles of healing would spread like wildfire? Of course, He did. He knows all that has ever been, and all that will ever be. What Jesus knew in fact, was that the people of God had long-awaited their story of rescue and redemption. He also knew the desperation in their hearts might make them look in the wrong places and for the wrong things.

Instead, Jesus consistently let His teaching and His miracles demonstrate that He was fulfilling all the Old Testament Prophecies for the Messiah.

Regarding these commands of Jesus to go and tell no one, St. Chrysostom said, "it is evident that He wished to draw the thoughts of man away from His miracles, and to fix them upon His doctrine." (2)

In many of the passages we've read, even though Jesus has miraculously healed these people, and then given them strict instructions not to tell anyone about it, many of them began immediately sharing that they'd been healed. How does that make you feel?

Imagine for a moment that you were in their position. Do you think it would be easy to obey the command, because of what Jesus had done, or do you think it would be hard to keep the command because you'd want to share it?

What is God stirring up in your heart, after reading this today?

Day 4

Do you ever read a passage of Scripture, or even just a sentence and say to yourself, "has that ALWAYS been in there?! I feel like I am seeing that for the first time!"

If you feel like that today, I am totally withyou.

I'll never forget the first time I began to look up and write down just how many times Jesus had an encounter with someone and then said, "go and tell no one." Today, we'll look at yet another passage that describes a quickly developing pattern at this stage of the unfolding ministry of Jesus. Let's open our Bibles and read Luke 4:40-44.

Luke 4:40-44 (NIV)
40 At sunset, the people brought to Jesus all who had various kinds of sickness, and laying His hands on each one, He healed them. 41 Moreover, demons came out of many people, shouting, "You are the Son of God!" But He rebuked them and would not allow them to speak, because they knew He was the Messiah. 42 At daybreak, Jesus went out to a solitary place. The people were looking for Him and when they came to where He was, they tried to keep Him from leaving them. 43 But He said, "I must proclaim the good news of the kingdom of God to the other towns also, because that is why I was sent." 44 And He kept on preaching in the synagogues of Judea.

In preparing this Bible Study, I have probably read each of these verses hundreds of times. For some reason, when I read this particular passage, and specifically the words of Jesus, I often get a little choked up. Maybe because we see here, what Jesus must have really been feeling during these interactions, and it this point in His growing ministry.

Read again the words of Luke 4:42, and write out the words of Jesus in Luke 4:43.

What does it make you feel when you read those words of Jesus?

What do you think that Jesus, in His heart of hearts, wanted to offer His people?

And based on this passage, what do you think the people were interested in?

I promise we won't do this EVERY time, but I think it can be so insightful to read these words, with a close translation from the original text, but in a heart language that is close to our own. So, let's look at this passage in *the Message* translation, as well:

Luke 4:40-44 The Message (MSG)
40-41 When the sun went down, everyone who had anyone sick with some ailment or other brought them to Him. One by one He placed His hands on them and healed them. Demons left in droves, screaming, "Son of God! You're the Son of God!" But He shut them up, refusing to let them speak because they knew too much, knew Him to be the Messiah.
42-44 He left the next day for open country. But the crowds went looking and, when they found Him, clung to Him so He couldn't go on. He told them, "Don't you realize that there are yet other villages where I have to tell the Message of God's Kingdom, that this is the work God sent me to do?"

In a day and age like ours, we are used to things "going viral." It looks like maybe we didn't even need computers or iPhones or social media for that.

Is it possible, that as a whole, we the people, have always been drawn to the "sensational?" And is it possible that the only thing we love more than the shock and awe, is when we get to experience that for ourselves, and then we get to share it?

What do you think it is, in the heart of a human being that is drawn to that sort of thing?

In this passage, we finally get a glimpse of the God-in-man, Jesus, spending His life spreading the good news of the New Covenant and the gospel of truth, and grace and freedom. *We get a glimpse of how frustrating it must have been for Jesus to be offering New Life, freedom from bondage, forgiveness of sin, and complete Healing and restoration with the Father, through a relationship with Him, and all the people wanted was one-stop-shop-healing for their ailments.* We get the sense that the crowds surrounding Jesus were lined up, solely for the transaction. They seemed to be concerned only with what He could do for them, in the moment. Does that resonate withyou, at all today? Have you ever found yourself more interested in having Jesus just answer your prayer, rather than listening to what He is longing to teach you and offer you?

Write your thoughts on that here...

Day 5

I'm not sure it was common back in the days of Jesus, but did you know there are entire fields of study, within Psychology and Sociology, that look at the phenomenon of crowds, and the forming of messages and media. Amazingly, subjects like "Crowd Psychology" and the "Psychology of Viral Content" are being studied and written about right now, in our culture. In some recent studies, one researcher concluded that "one of the things that is fundamental to human nature is that we imitate the actions of those around us." She goes on to say that, "in study after study, it turns out that cues in their environment are a strong determining factor in what actions people take." (3)

So, it isn't surprising that whether it's people in a large crowd, jumping on the bandwagon and participating in whatever behavior they see present, or a meme or video on social media that goes viral, so often we take our cues from the things we see other people doing. Have you seen how people react when the news says there could *possibly* be a shortage of gasoline? Or have you ever been to the grocery store bread aisle a few hours after the T.V. meteorologists predict a serious storm threatening to hit your area? I know I am guilty of getting wrapped up in the frenzy! And it certainly isn't a bad thing to be prepared…it's just funny to think about how certain things truly tend to spread like wildfire.

It is interesting, isn't it…? The life and times when Jesus was walking the earth, were certainly different in almost every way from what we know. But that thing inside us…that "crowd phenomenon" … it looks like it has been there in the hearts of humanity for generations and generations, dating back thousands of years.

Let's take another look at the passages from God's Word that we read earlier this week. Read both **Mark 7:31-37** and **Luke 4:40-44**.

Use any version you like, and read it again and write down any specific observations you have about what was going on within the larger groups of people present in both passages. Choose one of the methods described in the Appendix, or another set of tools that helps you study inductively.

Observations from Mark 7:31-37:

Observations from Luke 4:40-44:

So, here is the part where I want us to get really honest.

It's easy to read these passages and stay removed from them, and read them simply as a historical account that happened one day, a long time ago. But like we read on Day 1 this week, I want us to practice that type of "exegesis," where we read the text, gain truth and clarity on the precise context and content of the words, and then let the words "read us."

David, the Shepherd King, and the man after God's own heart, models for us the most beautiful heart posture in the well-known **Psalm 139.**

Interestingly, he begins with,

1 "O Lord, you have searched me and you know me. 2 You know when I sit and when I rise; you perceive my thoughts from afar. 3 You discern my going out and my lying down; you are familiar with all my ways. 4 Before a word is on my tongue you know it completely, O Lord."

And in a beautiful posture of humility, he ends with,

23 "Search me, O God, and know my heart; test me and know my anxious thoughts. 24 See if there is any offensive way in me, and lead me in the way everlasting."

We'll talk more about this prayer later because I truly think it is one of the most profound and powerful passages in Scripture, but today I just want us to take a cue from David and position our hearts in that same way.

There is an acknowledgment in His spirit that says, "Lord…you already know my heart. I don't even have to say out loud what I'm thinking, and you already know. Lord, would you reveal and bring into the light all that I am holding deep within my own heart. If I'm not saying it out loud, maybe I am not even aware of the longings deep in my heart.

Would you help me to identify thoughts or tendencies or even strongholds that guide my words and my actions?"

Imagine yourself in the crowd that day, in the presence of Jesus. Imagine seeing Him, face to face and watching as He opens the eyes of the blind, makes the deaf to hear and the lame to walk. With all the transparency you can muster, ask yourself this...

"Would my first instinct be to bow down in worship, as I hang on to every word the Master Teacher says, or would my first instinct possibly be to think of what He could do for me... what problem of mine that He could fix with a single word or touch of His hand.

Write your thoughts here...

Day 6/ Remember

Lord, I remember again today that I have everything I need in Your Word. And as I read Scripture this week, I remember, again, how you came to preach the Kingdom of God to us.

With the posture I see modeled in the heart of David in Psalm 139, I come before you Lord, asking you to search me and examine my heart. Open my eyes to see Your truth and remind me what is true.

If I am honest, do I see myself in the crowds pressing in around Jesus, wanting only my own needs to be met? Do I often come before you, caring less about what you are seeking to teach and stir up in me, and instead sticking closely to my own agenda for You to bring relief to whatever tension or pain or crisis that I am feeling in the moment?

Lord, if I truly know You, and understand who You are, then my heart would be not so easily drawn to *just* what You can do for me. How often do I miss a powerful and sacred encounter withyou Jesus, because I am too busy asking what You can do for me, instead?

And Lord, would You teach me and bring to my remembrance the truth that sometimes my obedience to what You are asking in my life, is not just about what You are doing in my life, but also what You are doing in the larger story. Remind me that I can trust You, above all else, even when I don't understand.

When I read Your word, I remember again, that Your heart for me is not just that I would know You simply as the one who answers my prayers and requests. Your Word helps me to remember again the beauty and freedom I find both in seeing You, for who You are, and in the message, You came to proclaim. Today Jesus, I remember that You are my Healer, but also my Rescuer, my Savior, my Redeemer, my Friend and my Lord. I don't know what I would have done, if I had been among the people in the crowd, pressing in on You as You healed the sick, and gave sight to the blind, but today I will choose to worship You, and sit and enjoy the beauty of who You are, Jesus.

Lord, after reading and studying this week, I *remember* again who You are, and what I most feel You stirring up in me is…

Today, Lord I want to really remember, and to rest in the Secret and Sacred with you, and this is the prayer of my heart…

Psalm 77:11
I will remember the deeds of the Lord;
yes, I will remember your wonders of old.

Day 7/ Rest

Lord, as I read back over what I've learned from Your Word this week, I acknowledge and identify the truths and concepts that You brought into the light. I am taking time to pay attention to what You are stirring up in me.

I want to remember and rest in the words I read in the passages this week. This is the overflow of my heart today...

I am reminded again of the words in 2 Timothy, that tell me that Your Word is" useful for teaching, rebuking, correcting and training in righteousness, so that the servant of God may be thoroughly equipped for every good work." Jesus, I invite You to use Your Word to teach me and to correct me... I position myself before You and ask these questions... Do I ever find myself with the same posture that many of the people in the crowds surrounding Jesus might have had? Do I ever approach, You God, with a list of requests, hoping that You'll wave some sort of magic wand and fix whatever my need is in that moment...?

And if that is true, is it possible that in doing that, I end up forfeiting an amazing encounter withyou, Jesus? Do I miss the sacred opportunity to see You, hear You, learn from You, and enjoy You, because I am more focused on what You can DO for me, rather than WHO You already are?

Remind me, Lord, that just as it was true in many encounters in the gospels, my own personal obedience may not *just* have to do with my own story, but quite possibly what You are also doing in Your larger story, that I can't even see yet?

Would You help me to remember Lord, that either way…I can rest in knowing that You are always working, and I can trust You with my obedience, even if I don't understand. Lord help me listen, to hear You, and to pay attention to what You are stirring in me, as I respond in faith and obedience.

Lord, this is my prayer for today:

Lord, I come to You in the spirit of confession and acknowledge that I am often like the people we read about this week when I:

Jesus, today I want to stop and remember so that I can rest in who You are, and what I know to be true of You.

When I know and remember….

I can rest in....

Jesus, in light of what I have learned this week, and as I position my heart to Remember and Rest in the Secret and the Sacred, this is my prayer...

Week 3

Day 1

So far, we've read several accounts where Jesus had a life-changing interaction with some-one and then said, "Go and tell no one." We've seen how the news about what Jesus could do, spread throughout the whole region and crowds began to follow Jesus every-where He went. Today we will continue to look at some of the interactions of Jesus during this time of His emerging public ministry.

Open your Bible, and let's read a beautiful passage in Luke.

Luke 8:40-56 (HCSB)

40 When Jesus returned, the crowd welcomed Him, for they were all expecting Him. 41 Just then, a man named Jairus came. He was a leader of the synagogue. He fell down at Jesus' feet and pleaded with Him to come to his house, 42 because he had an only daughter about 12 years old, and she was at death's door. While He was going, the crowds were nearly crushing Him. 43 A woman suffering from bleed-ing for 12 years, who had spent all she had on doctors yet could not be healed by any, 44 approached from behind and touched the tassel of His robe. Instantly her bleeding stopped. 45 "Who touched Me?" Jesus asked. When they all denied it, Peter said, "Master, the crowds are hemming You in and pressing against You." 46 "Someone did touch Me," said Jesus. "I know that power has gone out from Me." 47 When the woman saw that she was discovered, she came trembling and fell down before Him. In the presence of all the people, she declared the reason she had touched Him and how she was instantly cured.
48 "Daughter," He said to her, "your faith
has made you well. Go in peace."
49 While He was still speaking, someone came from
the synagogue leader's house, saying, "Your daugh-
ter is dead. Don't bother the Teacher anymore."
50 When Jesus heard it, He answered him, "Don't be afraid. Only believe, and she will be made well." 51 After He came to the house, He let no one enter with Him except Peter, John, James, and the child's father and mother. 52 Everyone was crying and mourning for her. But He said, "Stop crying, for she is not dead but asleep." 53 They started laughing at Him, because they knew she was dead. 54 So He took her by the hand and called out, "Child, get up!" 55 Her spirit returned, and she got up at once. Then He gave orders that she be given something to eat. Her parents were astounded, but *He instructed them to tell no one what had happened.*

This passage tells two separate, but parallel stories. See the <u>Appendix</u> for a list of inductive study methods, or use whatever method is already your favorite, to write down the context, taking note of what was happening in both stories.

Compare and contrast all the parts each of the stories; the healing of the woman, as well as the interaction between Jesus, and Jairus and his daughter. Make a note about the setting and who was present at each interaction.

What is similar in both interactions?

What is different in the interactions?

What do you learn about Jesus in each story?

Day 2

In week 1, we talked about how the "Synoptic Gospels," Matthew, Mark, and Luke, often include the same stories, but each gosple gives us its own details and summary of an event. That is certainly the case in the telling of the story about the woman with "the issue of blood," as well as the healing of Jairus' daughter.

Yesterday we read **Luke 8:40-56**. You can find the same story in **Matthew 9:18-26**, as well as **Mark 5:21-43**.

Today, I want us to engage in that practice of using God's Word, to illuminate God's Word! If we know where to look, and how to put the puzzle pieces together, we can get such a full picture of each of these interactions without even using any other sources! Refer to the Appendix and take note of how some Bible translations are "word for word" translations, some are "thought for thought" translations, and some are paraphrases. Each type of text is so important, and when we are analyzing a passage for study, it can be so helpful to see how each type of translation brings its own depth and clarity.

Read **Matthew 9:18-26**, and **Mark 5:21-43**, and compare them with the passage from yesterday, in **Luke 8:40-56**. You may use all three gospel re-tellings, in Matthew, Mark, and Luke, and you may use any translations you like, as long as you are only using Scripture! Fill in as many gaps as possible, and record your insights here...

Using whatever inductive study method you like, write down any new observations or insights about the people involved, the setting, and what you learn about Jesus...

I have come to love and savor Eugene Peterson's translation of Scripture in the Message. He is both a pastor, and an experienced professor in the original Biblical languages, and his translation is considered a paraphrase, which differs somewhat from traditional translations. Because of his background and expertise, he gives us a unique perspective that is so helpful in identifying the integrity and the intent of the original languages, while associating them with modern everyday English. With that in mind, let's cap off our study of this passage today, by reading this story in the Message.

Luke 8:40-56, MSG

40-42 On his return, Jesus was welcomed by a crowd. They were all there expecting Him. A man came up, Jairus by name. He was president of the meeting place. He fell at Jesus' feet and begged Him to come to his home because his twelve-year-old daughter, his only child, was dying. Jesus went with him, making His way through the pushing, jostling crowd. 43-45 In the crowd that day there was a woman who for twelve years had been afflicted with hemorrhages. She had spent every penny she had on doctors but not one had been able to help her. She slipped in from behind and touched the edge of Jesus' robe. At that very moment her hemorrhaging stopped. Jesus said, "Who touched me?" When no one stepped forward, Peter said, "But Master, we've got crowds of people on our hands. Dozens have touched you." 46 Jesus insisted, "Someone touched me. I felt power discharging from me." 47 When the woman realized that she couldn't remain hidden, she knelt trembling before Him. In front of all the people, she blurted out her story—why she touched Him and how at that same moment she was healed. 48 Jesus said, "Daughter, you took a risk trusting me, and now you're healed and whole. Live well, live blessed!" 49 While he was still talking, someone from the leader's house came up and told him, "Your daughter died. No need now to bother the Teacher." 50-51 Jesus overheard and said, "Don't be upset. Just trust me and everything will be all right." Going into the house, He wouldn't let anyone enter with Him except Peter, John, James, and the child's parents. 52-53 Everyone was crying and carrying on over her. Jesus said, "Don't cry. She didn't die; she's sleeping." They laughed at Him. They knew she was dead. 54-56 Then Jesus, gripping her hand, called, "My dear child, get up." She was up in an instant, up and breathing again! He told them to give her something to eat. Her parents were ecstatic, but Jesus warned them to keep quiet. "Don't tell a soul what happened in this room."

Read this passage several times today. What is God stirring up in you today, after reading and studying?

Day 3

So, we haven't even looked at any outside sources, but look at all that we have learned! I hope it feels gratifying to you, to realize how much wisdom we can uncover for ourselves when we study God's Word!

Today I want to keep adding puzzle pieces and putting them together. We'll aim to get more of a clear and full picture, by still only using God's Word, but by looking to see what treasures are tucked away in the original language of these sections of Scripture. I have always been fascinated and drawn to understanding the original languages, but it wasn't until a few years ago that I realized how easy it was to find access to simple word translations to help in my own understanding of a passage. Please know that I am NOT saying that the Greek and Hebrew languages are easy… they are actually quite different from our patterns in English and take years of intense study to master. What I am hoping to convey here, is that with readily available and helpful tools, it can be really easy to find an accurate translation for an English word in our Scripture passages, from the original language translation, with its intended use, tense and context. I'll never forget learning how using some simple tools would seem to take a word or two from a straightforward, black and white verse, to what felt like 3-D, High Definition, Color! Sometimes our English translations are completely accurate, but we don't seem to get *the depth* of what is being conveyed in the meanings of the original Greek words in New Testament, and Hebrew words in the Old Testament.

If this is a new practice for you, I'd love to show you how easy it is!

Using whatever tools you have available, consider doing a word study on the original Greek words used in this passage for "heal" or "healed" or "made well," (depending on what version you are using.) The insights from the original language are invaluable in understanding the progression of the words used in this woman's journey to find healing in **Luke 8:40-48**.

If you have access to a Key Word Study Bible, a Strong's Exhaustive Concordance of the Bible, or a Vine's Complete Expository Dictionary of the Old and New Testaments, do some digging and see what you can figure out about the words used in this passage.

If you don't have access to these, try doing an online search. (Seriously…it's really easy!) Type into your search bar, "Interlinear Bible, Luke 8" and you'll be directed to biblehub.com or another similar resource, that will show you the direct translations from the Greek words originally used in the New Testament, with their definitions, and grammatical information. Strong's Exhaustive Concordance assigns numbers to each of the original language words, which can be used in searching for original language definitions and their English translations.

There are several ways to look into the original language wordings. Try doing some research on your own and write down any insights you find here...

It is so endearing that it's actually the gospel writer Luke, who was also a physician, that gives us specific details about the progression of her healing when we look at the original Greek words used here. He records that, even after this woman spent her entire living on seeking treatment, his fellow physicians were not ever able to cure her of her disease (from the Greek word, "therapeuo," #2323, in Luke 8:43). (1) Luke goes on to record her encounter with Jesus and describes how her faith in Jesus is what ultimately brought instant healing to her body (from the Greek word, "iaomai," #2390, in Luke 8:47). (2) Luke also further specifies how *her faith in Jesus* not only made her well, but restored her, saved her and brought ultimate healing to both her *body and soul* (from the Greek word, "sozo," #4982, in Luke 8:50). (3)

This is a rich and powerful passage, that deserves an extended time in study because of what it teaches us about Jesus. We see the woman, longing for the healing touch of Jesus, secretly, and desperately reaching out, in faith for the fringe of His robe. And then Jesus, after hearing her declaration "in the presence of all the people," calling her "daughter," and publicly affirming that it was her faith that made her well. And the parallel progression of the story of Jairus, and his daughter is equally intriguing. Jairus, a powerful official of the synagogue, making a public plea for Jesus to come heal his daughter, interrupted by His encounter with the woman. The desperate and public plea from this powerful and influential man is ultimately also answered with complete healing, but behind closed doors, and followed by instructions to *"tell no one."* Read the passage again, and record any new observations you have about Jesus, and what He may be stirring up in you, as you read.

Day 4

Today we are going to begin by reading Matthew 16:13-20.

Matthew 16:13-20 (CSB)
**13 When Jesus came to the region of Caesarea Philippi, He asked
His disciples, "Who do people say that the Son of Man is?"
14 They replied, "Some say John the Baptist; others, Elijah;
still others, Jeremiah or one of the prophets."
15 "But you," He asked them, "who do you say that I am?"
16 Simon Peter answered, "You are the
Messiah, the Son of the living God."
17 Jesus responded, "Blessed are you, Simon son of Jonah, because flesh and blood did not reveal this to you, but my Father in
heaven. 18 And I also say to you that you are Peter, and on this rock
I will build my church, and the gates of Hades will not overpower
it. 19 I will give you the keys of the kingdom of heaven, and whatever you bind on earth will have been bound in heaven, and whatever you loose on earth will have been loosed in heaven." 20 Then He
gave the disciples orders to tell no one that he was the Messiah.**

This same passage is written about in **Mark 8:27-30**, and **Luke 9:18-21**, as well, if you would like to read those passages and compare them to Matthew's telling.

I've mentioned that my husband and I have a ministry called Withyou, and one of our most favorite offerings, is a retreat experience, where we follow the relationship between Jesus and Peter. It is a complex and layered story, and one of the most beautiful examples of how the true restoration that the gospel of Jesus offers, is based on His covenant with us, not our commitment to Him. I always love peeking in, and watching the progression of how the disciples grew with Jesus, as they began to follow Him, learn from Him, and ultimately become transformed by their intimate relationship with Him.

Interestingly, at this point, Peter and the other disciples whom Jesus called, had been following Him for quite some time. At first, the questions that Jesus asks His disciples in Matthew 16:13, and then again in 15 seem a little odd. But once we remember the way of Jesus, and how He so often asks questions to reveal what is going on deep down in our hearts, we see that He is looking to reveal the depth of the belief and understanding the disciples have, at this point in their journey with Him. Peter responds with as much Spirit-revealed wisdom as He can, at this point in the journey, saying, "You are the Messiah, the Son of the living God." In the Message version, we see that Jesus responded, "God bless you, Simon, son of Jonah! You didn't get that answer out of books or from teachers. My Father in heaven, God Himself, *let you in on this **secret** of who I really am.*"

What does this mean to you, and why do you think this interaction is important?

You might notice that, once again, Jesus gives the command, to *"tell no one"* about what happened. This particular interaction was not after a healing, but after an intimate and significant encounter, giving them more understanding of who Jesus really was. What happens immediately following the passage we just read, unfolds in a way that is completely fascinating. Read Matthew 16:21-23 (or all the way to v28).

Matthew 16:21-23 (CSB)

21 From then on Jesus began to point out to His disciples that it was necessary for Him to go to Jerusalem and suffer many things from the elders, chief priests, and scribes, be killed, and be raised the third day. 22 Peter took Him aside and began to rebuke Him, "Oh no, Lord! This will never happen to you!"
23 Jesus turned and told Peter, "Get behind me, Satan! You are a hindrance to me because you're not thinking about God's concerns but human concerns."
24 Then Jesus said to his disciples, "If anyone wants to follow after me, let him deny himself, take up his cross, and follow me. 25 For whoever wants to save his life will lose it, but whoever loses his life because of Me will find it. 26 For what will it benefit someone if he gains the whole world yet loses his life? Or what will anyone give in exchange for his life? 27 For the Son of Man is going to come with his angels in the glory of his Father, and then he will reward each according to what he has done. 28 Truly I tell you, there are some standing here who will not taste death until they see the Son of Man coming in his kingdom."

Using your own words, describe what happened between Jesus and Peter throughout the course of this interaction.

Day 5

In the interaction we read about yesterday, between Jesus and Peter, there is such irony, as it all unfolds. Read **Matthew 16:13-20** again today.

In this passage, we see Jesus praising Peter for his Holy Spirit-prompted insight, into the true identity of Jesus. And then immediately after that, in verses 21-28, we see some pretty strong language from Jesus, and the high praise of Peter is quickly replaced with a harsh reprimand. Write down your thoughts about the progression here…

Can you identify with Peter at all here?

What stirs up in you, when you hear the words of Jesus to Peter, *"Get behind Me, Satan! You are a stumbling block to Me; for you are not setting your mind on God's interests, but man's."*

What is it about us…? How do we sometimes identify, and even rest, in the upside-down Kingdom ways of Jesus one minute, and then in the next minute think that it must be all wrong? Our hearts are so prone to wander, and even more prone to forget what we already know to be true, aren't they? Why do we sometimes, take on this same spirit in Peter here, and try to fight or even correct the upside-down world of Jesus?

Jesus uses these moments to "state the matter plainly," as it says in Mark 8. So often, God intends to bring about His purposes in the exact OPPOSITE way we would have done it…and instead of leaning in and hanging on every word, sensing that we are being let in on the greatest plot twist ever written…why do we so often instead, assume that the ship is off course, and needs our help to get back on track?

Time and time again we see that the Kingdom of Jesus truly is upside down, and inside out and that His ways are not our ways. Why have we not come to trust it fully? And why do we so often forget?

It is a fascinating, and even enlightening progression to watch the disciples have this intimate encounter with Jesus. They already carried a deep knowledge of who Jesus was, but in this moment, it is deepened, even still. They knew Jesus to be the long-awaited Messiah, but they didn't fully understand what being the Messiah actually meant. Then, as the gospels tell us, "He warned the disciples that they should *tell no one* that He was the Christ." Jesus began to paint the picture for them, of just exactly what being the Messiah would mean… and how it would be necessary for Him to suffer, be rejected and even be killed, and raised up again, to bring about the reconciliation of God and man. And then Peter, with the praise from Jesus for his Spirit-given wisdom, still freshly on his ears, "took Him aside *and began to rebuke Him*, saying, "God forbid, it Lord! This shall never happen to You." Jesus is letting them in on His plan. And Peter, (who'd just been praised for hearing from the Father, Himself), hears what the painful, and heartbreaking journey for Jesus will look like, and actually *rebukes Jesus*, insisting that certainly, this must not be the plan.

I'm sure we'd all like to think that if we were sitting across from Jesus, and He used actual, audible words to spell out His perfect plan before us, that we'd listen approvingly and hang on every word. But how many of us, so often have this ever-changing heart of Peter and a faith like shifting sand? How often do our words say, "Lord, let Your will be done on earth, and in me," but what our hearts really mean, is "*as long as that's something I want to hear.*"

Take some time to read again, about this interaction between Jesus and Peter. We've looked at the passage a few times in Matthew 16:13-23. Remember that the other synoptic gospels give us this account, as well, in **Mark 8:27-33**, and **Luke 9:18-21**. What is God stirring up in you, as you read and reflect on this interaction?

Day 6/ Remember

Throughout the gospels, we get to peek inside the small windows that give us a glimpse of Jesus, bringing the Kingdom of God to earth. It wasn't flashy or showy, and although Jesus was the ultimate authority and power, He always communicated with humility, in perfect step with the Father. We continue to see, over and over, that the ways of Jesus are often not our ways. And we, like Peter, can find ourselves believing Him fully in one minute, and doubting His plan and His ways, the next.

When we find ourselves like a moth to a flame, and our hearts are magnetically drawn to ways of the world, we need to *remember Jesus*.

Why do we so often hear the heart of Jesus, but then take on the posture of Peter, in the passage we read? And even if we don't rebuke Jesus out loud, with our words, why do we so often rebuke, or correct Him, with the spirit in our heart, that is so insatiably drawn to the ways of the world, instead? Whether we say it out loud or not, how often do we join in the chorus of Peter, and the countless followers since Him, when we protest that there must be a better way? We might not even realize we are doing it, but sometimes the discomfort we feel in that upside-down world of Jesus, makes us feel like we need to turn it right side up. It doesn't often happen in an obvious way…I think we rarely open our mouths, and actually *tell God* that we think He is wrong, and that His ways are just not quite right. But our affections give us away. Like Peter, we may hear from God clearly. But how often do we find ourselves following Jesus, and then realize we've followed Him outside of the known, familiar path, away from the comforts we are accustomed to, and so we assume then, that something must be wrong?

Just like Peter, our hearts betray us, when we follow Jesus with zeal and devotion *until* we see the great cost of following Him may mean taking up our own cross, leading us in a constant uphill battle with the world. Our hearts are so often tightly wrapped up in our own desires to be happy, secure, comfortable, affirmed, and valued. Our affections for a seemingly good, happy, purposeful, and meaningful life, end up shaping some of our deepest hopes. With our minds, and our mouths, we declare a desire to walk in the ways of Jesus, but deep in our hearts, we are pulled by our own desires, shaped by what the world loves and values.

What are some areas, where you find yourself like Peter, in step with Jesus in one moment, and then find yourself, suggesting a better way, in the next?

When we are prone to wander and gravitate towards a path that brings the ease of comfort, accolades because of our actions, and honor because of influence, may we find ourselves here… gazing on Jesus, the Healing Messiah, the Curious Savior, intimately stepping into the lives of those He loved. Jesus often drew close those that others disregarded, changing their lives forever, but asking those He'd changed, to tell no one about it.

When we find ourselves celebrating, and loving what the world loves, may we turn our hearts to remember Jesus.

When we look at the ways that Jesus chose to live, and move and speak, may we *remember again*, the upside-down ways of His Kingdom.
May we identify and confess when the longings of our hearts give our natural allegiances away. When our attractions and our affections begin to lean towards what the world sees as valuable and right, we knit ourselves to a false gospel. In this day and age, the specifics may look a bit differently than they did for Peter and the other disciples. In our culture today, as believers, our biggest struggles may not be easily visible or obvious. I wonder how often our biggest struggles land in that gray area between the ways of Jesus and the ways of the world?

Sometimes in our culture, it feels like the message is, "louder, wider, higher, and farther!" We often hear a message that encourages that "influence can make you a better steward," "fame can give you a bigger platform," and "momentum can help spread your message." And, there are moments that may be right. *Absolutely.* But when we get so wrapped up in the ways of the world, that we rebuke the heart of Jesus by placing our affection, our longing and our stamp of approval there, and only there, we miss everything that Jesus was about. We forget that Jesus totally had the option to go big, to go loud, to choose power, and to value the public moments over the private ones. *He had the option to choose that.* But time and time again, the gospels paint the picture of Jesus in beautiful, everyday moments, investing in those closest to Him, inviting in those that the world discarded, and giving value to sacred encounters, often between just Himself and one or two other people. His ways were upside down, and opposite, and when it seemed like a time to go and tell, He so often said, *"go and tell no one."* If we learn anything from these gospel passages, I pray that God will seal in our hearts and help us remember, *the Kingdom ways of Jesus... often small, beautifully intimate, and sometimes secret.* What is Jesus asking you to remember again, today?

Day 7/ Rest

Today, Jesus, I lay my heart open before You. I confess that I sometimes believe You with my words, but rebuke You in my heart.

I know you are not surprised when I am unsure about Your upside-down Kingdom ways, but I also know that You are always there saying,

"My presence will go withyou, and I will give you rest." (Exodus 33:14)

Jesus, this is the overflow of my heart today…

Jesus, I invite You again to use Your Word to teach me and to correct me… I position myself before you and to wrestle through and confess when I sometimes find myself in the posture of Peter, following You with my words, but secretly rebuking You deep inside my heart.

Lord, today I lay before you…

As I reflect on our reading this week, I remember the two parallel encounters withyou, Jesus. One began with desperation, and in secret, but ended with a public declaration and faith that brought healing. The other began with a public plea, but ended with a secret, sacred encounter, bringing ultimate healing, but behind closed doors, away from the crowd.

Jesus, help me to know and follow Your heart. Help me to remember and rest in knowing that I can trust You as my Healer, my Savior, my Redeemer, and Friend. Remind me that, in following You, I may find myself in "go and tell" moments, declaring in the presence of the people, all that You have done for me. And also help me to rest and remember, that You some-times call me to, "go and tell no one moments," that are *sacred and beautiful and just for You and me*. Help me to value and celebrate both. Help me to remember the upside-down ways of Your Kingdom, Jesus.

When the world would have me value, what is visible and measurable, help me to rest in the Secret and the Sacred, of intimate encounters withyou.

Even when I forget, bring to my remembrance, Psalm 51:6, as the cry of my heart.

Psalm 51:6 (ESV)
Behold, You delight in truth in the inward being,
and You teach me wisdom in the secret heart.

Jesus, today I want to remember and rest in who You are, and what I already know to be true of You.

When I know and remember…

I can rest in…

Jesus, in light of what I have learned this week, and as I position my heart to Remember and Rest in the Secret and the Sacred, this is my prayer….

Psalm 116:7
Return to your rest, my soul,
for the Lord has been good to you.

Week 4

Day 1

*C*ongratulations! We are halfway through our study on learning to Remember and Rest in the Secret and the Sacred. The first three weeks we spent diving deep into Scripture Passages in the gospels, looking at several important encounters of Jesus. For the last half of our study, we'll continue to build our foundation on the Word of God, and we'll spend some time asking God to search our hearts. We'll pay attention to what He is stirring up in us, as we build the application bridge from Scripture to our own lives today.

The basis for our study is to look deep into the gospels and to pay specific attention to the many times that Jesus says, "Go and tell no one." We've established that much of the reason that Jesus said those words in those specific interactions had to do with the way His public ministry was unfolding, and even more so, about the condition of the hearts of His people as they were beginning to understand who Jesus really was. We know that it was important to Jesus that people spend time listening to His teaching, and understanding the gospel He preached, to more fully be able to receive Him as their Messiah and Savior. We know historically, that the people of God in the days of Jesus, were desperate for a ruler and King to rescue them in power from the oppression they had suffered at the hands of the Roman Empire. We also know from specific gospel accounts that the people Jesus was trying to reach with His message, (including the disciples), didn't fully understand who Jesus was, and certainly didn't fully understand His mission and purpose. There was undeniable wisdom and even supernatural power in this Man that could heal the sick, and open the eyes of the blind. But Jesus truly saw into the hearts of His people and knew that they didn't understand that His mission was not to come and rescue them politically, or even simply to bring healing. He had come to change their lives forever, but not in the ways they were expecting. He didn't come for just one people, or for just one time. He had come to save the souls of all men, to forgive them of sin, and make a way to a Sinless and Perfect God, once and for all. He knew their desperation, and their tendency to gravitate towards *what* Jesus could do for them, instead of understanding *who* He was.

I imagine that tendency is one that still resonates with us today. Just as Jesus knew the hearts of the people walking beside Him during His time on earth, He knows our hearts today, as well. We are going to spend some time this week, asking God to search our hearts, and even reveal to us the truth of what He sees there. We'll spend some time pondering, and looking deep within ourselves to answer some of the deeper questions God is stirring in our hearts.

We see all throughout Scripture, that even for the followers of Jesus, it took a long time to fully see a full picture of who He truly was.

I get that. Don't you? As many years as I've loved and followed Jesus, I know that there are parts of His nature and character that I've seen clearly and that there are also parts that I've only just begun to see and understand. The older I get, the more I'm able to clearly see that my vantage point, as I walk this life, is limited, and marked by the mysteries of Christ. I'm keenly aware that Jesus sees and knows all. There is a beautiful humility that comes when we surrender to the fact that we don't know the whole story…we can't see all that God is doing, and even when He pulls back the curtain to give us glimpses of all that He is doing, we still can only know what He reveals. We know that is true in our lives today, just as it was true in the stories we read of Jesus, and His disciples and those that followed Him during His ministry here on earth. As much as we'd so often like to think that we have a grasp on things, we are positioned only to really watch what unfolds before us. Sometimes we get to see that clearly, and sometimes we see God in the mystery, and that He is working in ways we don't yet see or understand.

We'll look more into that this week, but let's begin by looking at one last time in Scripture where we see this happening. We see Jesus pulling back the veil of heavenly, Kingdom things, but then giving instructions to those present, not to tell anyone about it, just yet.

Read the passage of Scripture that we call "the Transfiguration."
It is recorded in **Matthew 17: 1-13**, **Mark 9:2-13**, as well as **Luke 9:28-36**. Choose one of the passages, to read repeatedly, and study inductively, making observations about the encounter, and then, record your thoughts here.

Day 2

Let's begin today by thinking about the passage we read yesterday, as well as the many "go and tell no one" passages we've read in the last weeks.

We have the unusual perspective to look at these encounters with the knowledge of the whole story, and what is to come. We already know all that Jesus taught us about Himself, and we already know about His journey to the cross, and His victory over sin and death. As observers, we've already seen what comes on the pages that follow. We are able to see these interactions in light of who Jesus is, but we can appreciate how in the moment, as they happen, the story is still unfolding, and each of the people in these "go and tell no one" interactions are still putting the puzzle pieces together about who Jesus really is.

Take a few minutes to look back through the interactions we've read about in the last few weeks, taking note of the times we see Jesus letting people in on something miraculous and holy, but how they are still only able to understand it, *in part*. Once again, we see Jesus giving the command not to tell anyone what they'd seen. Does it make any more sense to you today?

Record your thoughts here.

Choose any "go and tell no one" passage that we have read together so far, and take a minute to imagine a bit more specifically what it would have been like for the person (or people) on the other side of the interaction with Jesus. What do you think they knew about Jesus at that point?

What do you imagine they might have felt or thought after their interaction with Jesus?

Try to imagine what it would have felt like to have the interaction, but then to have Jesus say, "go and tell no one." What do you think you would have felt, and do you think you would have been able to obey the command?

Think for a moment about the concept that sometimes Jesus is working in ways we cannot fully see and understand, and that sometimes our vantage point only gives us clarity, in part. Sometimes Jesus is working clearly in us, but sometimes He is working in His much larger story, as well. As we step back and look at the stories we've read in the gospels, we see that to be true, don't we? Jesus is bringing healing, restoration, forgiveness and life-changing grace to each situation, and to each individual person's life…we can see that. But He was also working in the *Secret Places* of a much larger Kingdom story, as well.

Take a minute to think about times that may have happened in your own life, and relationship with God.

Have there been times that you've seen Him step into your own life, and situation and you've seen Him work, but then only *later* did you see the *full* picture of how He was working? As you look back now, have there been times that Jesus was working in the *Secret Place*…in ways that you couldn't specifically see then, but can see now?

When you think back on that, is it possible that if you were to have told someone about what God was doing at the time, that you wouldn't have been able to tell the whole story? Write your thoughts here.

Day 3

Let's start today by reading some important words of Jesus in Matthew 6. If we look inductively at this passage and consider the placement, we see that it sits right in the middle of Jesus' Sermon on the Mount. To honor and appreciate these words, let's consider them in their context. Jesus began His sermon in Matthew 5, by establishing that righteousness was a gift of God's grace, and what our lives would look like, if we follow Him, and live from a deep, personal, genuine, satisfying relationship with Him, based on Christ's indwelling in us. This righteousness would no longer be something to strive for through good deeds and righteous acts, as had been the case for the people of God before Jesus. If you think about it, it had been possible for a Jewish follower of God, to appear holy and righteous on the outside, by displaying good deeds, while his heart could remain far from God on the inside. Now, in this new covenant of Jesus, we are each made righteous through Jesus alone, as evidenced by the true condition of our heart (not what it looks like on the outside). The entire Sermon on the Mount is well worth a thorough study on its own.

Today, let's look specifically at the words of Jesus in Matthew 6:1-8.

Matthew 6:1-8 (ESV)

6 "Beware of practicing your righteousness before other people in order to be seen by them, for then you will have no reward from your Father who is in heaven.

2 "Thus, when you give to the needy, sound no trumpet before you, as the hypocrites do in the synagogues and in the streets, that they may be praised by others. Truly, I say to you, they have received their reward. 3 But when you give to the needy, do not let your left hand know what your right hand is doing, 4 so that your giving may be in secret. And your Father who sees in secret will reward you.

5 "And when you pray, you must not be like the hypocrites. For they love to stand and pray in the synagogues and at the street corners, that they may be seen by others. Truly, I say to you, they have received their reward. 6 But when you pray, go into your room and shut the door and pray to your Father who is in secret. And your Father who sees in secret will reward you.

7 "And when you pray, do not heap up empty phrases as the Gentiles do, for they think that they will be heard for their many words. 8 Do not be like them, for your Father knows what you need before you ask Him."

In all of our "go and tell no one" passages, Jesus is essentially asking the person to keep their encounter a secret, and here in Matthew 6, Jesus speaks at great length about what should be done "in secret." Let's look at that more closely in Matthew 6.

What does Jesus say NOT to do, and why?

What does He say to do instead, and why?

In some translations, Jesus says that when we "give alms," which is defined as the act of fulfilling a material need for someone less fortunate (1), to do it "in secret." The actual Greek translation there, for "secret" comes from the word "kruptos," meaning "hidden, concealed, secret." What do you think that means in this context, and why do you think He gave these instructions?

Once again, we see Jesus getting right to the condition of our hearts. Here He is warning against *doing right things with the wrong motive*. What would be a wrong motive, and how would doing things "in secret" guard against that?

In verse 2, He says, "when you do a charitable deed" or "give alms," do not sound a trumpet. I'm not sure there are not too many people actually sounding trumpets to draw the attention of others to their good deeds, but there are plenty of other ways that we might do that, aren't there? ("To toot our own horn?"). If we let our defenses down and take that Psalm 139 heart posture of, "Search me O God," and ask Him to reveal what is in the deepest part of our hearts, what would He find there? Even if it is difficult, it's worth asking, "is there any part of me that wants my relationship with God, and my walk with Him to be a way for me to be seen, to be valued, to be applauded? Do I want to be seen and known as godly, and righteous?"

Here is where we get to "the root of the root." Obviously, God's heart for us IS to be holy, godly and righteous. He has set us apart for holiness. The subtle difference here lies solely in *our motive*. Am I wanting to *be holy* because *Christ is holy*, and I want to be *with Christ*? Or, do I want others to *see* me as holy, godly and righteous? Do I want to be seen and known for my part in that? Spend some time praying and asking God to reveal and bring to light what He is stirring deep in your heart. Write your thoughts here…

Day 4

Yesterday we had a chance to let God's Word reveal and uncover what is deep in our hearts. And today, we are going back in for more. Read the words of **Matthew 6:1-8** again, today.

We are going to continue *looking at the original language* used in these passages, to broaden our understanding of the words of Jesus. Only the Son of God, in human flesh, would for-see the longings and struggles deep within our hearts, and anticipate the need for this honest instruction. He knows us inside and out and better than we know ourselves. And He knows not only what we do, but why we do it! Only someone who knows our hearts so well would know to speak to the issue of doing the right thing in the sight of men, while actually carrying the wrong motive deep inside. Read Matthew 6: 1-8 again, choosing any version you like, and make a note of any new observations.

In chapter six, Jesus goes on speaking to the true condition of our hearts. Let's get the full picture by looking at the original language in this passage. In addition to using Strong's numbering system, another easy way to do this is by looking at the passage in an "Interlinear Bible" or by simply doing an online search. (Seriously…go to your search bar and type in, "Interlinear Bible Matthew 6" and you'll be directed to a great resource, like biblehub.com). You can see how the English words in our translations directly correspond to the original language, (Greek in this case.)

For example,

In Mt. 6:1, Jesus says, "Beware of practicing your righteousness before men *to be noticed by them.*" (Some versions say to "be seen by them.") When we look at the original Greek there, we see those words correlate with the Greek word "theaomai," which is Strong's Greek #2300. The word translates to the verb "*to behold, look upon, to perceive, to look closely.*" Using HELPS Word-studies further illuminates this for us, by including that "theaomai" is from "thaomai," meaning "*to gaze at a spectacle,*" properly, "*gaze on as a spectator.*" It is the root of the Greek word "theatron," meaning "*spectacle in a theatre,*" and is the root of the English term, "theater." (2)

So, the takeaway here is that the spirit of what Jesus was saying is something like, "when you are doing things for Me, *beware that it doesn't become a show!*"

Then, in verse 2, Jesus says, "don't sound a trumpet before you as the hypocrites do in the synagogues and in the streets that they may be honored by men." The word "hypocrite" used there is the word "hupokrites" in the Greek, and believe it or not, it actually translates to "an actor under an assumed character." In older Greek, a hypocrites ('hypocrite') was an actor, but by the first century, the term came to be used for those who play roles and see the world as their stage. Such performers are rightly called hypocrites, because they are actors, acting the part of pious, holy people when they are not. (3)

It's almost as if Jesus is anticipating the natural course that the heart of a believer may go on, (*even if it begins with a desire to please God,*) thinking something like, "if this is something Jesus wants me to do, I'll do it really well, and really boldly, and maybe even in a way that everyone can see what I'm about!"

Jesus addresses the danger that is possible deep in the heart of a believer to create an "image" of righteousness. An image that may have its roots in the desire to be noticed and applauded, like an actor performing on a stage in a theater, rather than in the desire to please God alone, *in secret,* where only He would know. Have you ever struggled with that tension? If so, explain.

It's all about the purpose for those good works, or "acts of righteousness" being seen in the first place. Matthew 5:16 says, "let your light so shine before others, so that they may see your good works and give glory to your Father who is in heaven." The tricky part there is remembering that the light shining, would be pointing to God, giving glory to our Father in heaven. If that light is shining back onto us, instead of the Father, then, in truth, we are seeking the glory for ourselves…not the glory of God, at all.

Wow! These words of Jesus have so much power to reveal things deep within and help us to examine our motives, for sure. Jesus is bringing challenge to the deepest parts of our heart, that hold our intent.

What is He stirring up in you, as you read His Words in this passage?

Day 5

Matthew 6 holds treasure beyond what our minds can comprehend. Let's look there again today. Yesterday, we read the words of Jesus warning us to look at the motive behind what we do for God and to guard against letting it become a show. Let's continue digging into that same passage, **Matthew 6:1-8**, and let's start by looking at verse 6.

Jesus says, "But when you pray, go into your inner room, and when you have shut your door, pray to your Father who is in secret, and your Father who sees in secret will repay you."

It can be so enlightening to look at the words in their original language and context. The Greek for "inner room" comes from "tameion" #5009, and means "an inner chamber," or a "secret chamber." (4) Not many of us have actual secret chambers tucked away in our homes, but what else could Jesus mean for us, in that?

Take another look at verse 6. Use your favorite inductive study method, or try one from the Appendix, to gain more clarity on the exact context, and write your observations here…

Jesus is giving us instructions on what it should look like when we pray to the Father. *Where does Jesus say that the Father is?*

We have spent a lot of time looking at the commands of Jesus to "go and tell no one," keeping encounters a secret, and to do things, "in secret." Now, Jesus is telling us that *the Father is IN THE SECRET.* What does that mean for us?

Jesus also tells us in both verse 4, and again here in verse 6, that, "your Father who sees in secret will repay you." What do you think He means when He says, *"your Father who sees in secret?"*

Let's look just a little bit further along in this passage, in Matthew 6:16-18.

> 16 "Whenever you fast, do not put on a gloomy face as the hypocrites
> do, for they neglect their appearance so that they will be noticed by men
> when they are fasting. Truly I say to you, they have their reward in full. 17
> But you, when you fast, anoint your head and wash your face 18 so that
> your fasting will not be noticed by men, but by your Father who is in se-
> cret; and your Father who sees what is done in secret will reward you."

Try using the Devotional Method (listed as "D." in the Appendix) to get some more clarity on this passage. Next week we'll look at what Jesus means when He talks about "rewards," but to-day, let's look at what His instructions are. Read and answer the Devotional Method questions, for example, "is there a sin to confess, a promise to claim, an attitude to change, a command to obey…etc."

When you look at the words of Jesus in this passage, do you see an attitude to change, a command to obey, or an example to follow or learn from?

What is at the root of this passage in the words of Jesus to the believer?

Jesus is clearly turning our hearts away from how we are perceived by those around us, and instead, drawing our hearts toward the Father, who is in secret.

Write down what Jesus is stirring up in you today...

Day 6 / Remember

It's so easy to forget to remember what we already know to be true. There are so many treasures that help us remember, hidden within the words of Jesus in the "go and tell no one" passages, as well as His words to us in Matthew 6. His words strongly urge us to take a look at what is going on deep within our hearts, and what the honest motive is behind our actions, especially in relation to spiritual things. Jesus invites us to look at the difference between what we do, that others can see, and what we do that only our Father, in Secret, can see. This echoes that familiar posture of the heart that we have studied in **Psalm 139**. To help us remember and rest, let's look at that one more time, and look even further to see how that might be related to our study this week. In week 2, we looked at how the Psalm opens with an invitation for God to "search my heart." There is even reference and acknowledgment in verse 15 when the Psalm reads,

> **My frame was *not hidden* from You,**
> **When I was made *in secret*,**

And interestingly, the Psalm closes with these words, in verses 23, 24.

> **Search me, O God, and know my heart;**
> **Try me and know my anxious thoughts;**
> **And see if there be any hurtful way in me,**
> **And lead me in the everlasting way.**

There are a couple of words that are used there, in verse 24. Some versions say "hurtful," some say "wicked." What is most insightful is not what our English word means, but rather what the Hebrew meaning is from the original translation. The Hebrew word used there is "otseb" (Strongs Hebrew #6090), which amazingly, means, "*idol*," or "a way of idolatry or error."

The unbelievable correlation comes from the connotation of the masculine noun, which indicates the pain and sorrow that come from toil, strife, and travail. It indicates the pain or hurtful way of any wicked habit. (5)

It is difficult, of course, to get the full picture in English, without knowing the complexities of Hebrew, but we can lean into the spirit of what is being said here, when we take that same posture of the Psalmist, and pray, "Search me, O God, and know my heart;

Try me and know my anxious thoughts; And see if there be any hurtful way in me…"

We can come before the Lord in that spirit, praying, "see if there is anything in my life that I've made an idol…is there anything that I have fashioned in pain or sorrow…is there any part of me that is holding on to something that is not your best for me?

Lord, after reading and studying Your words this week, is there a part of me that longs to be seen, valued and applauded by others? Do I forfeit a sacred encounter withyou in Secret, because I'd really rather bring it out to a public place to be seen and noticed by others?"

The Message translation of this passage offers us a beautiful prayer…

23-24 Investigate my life, O God,
find out everything about me;
Cross-examine and test me,
get a clear picture of what I'm about;
See for yourself whether I've done anything wrong—
then guide me on the road to eternal life.

Take a few minutes to prayerfully consider these words, and to listen to what Christ may be stirring up in you as you pray.

Pray, confess, listen, and write any thoughts here...

In closing today, we are going to look at one more word from the original language. In Matthew 6:4, Jesus talks about *"your Father who sees in secret."* The Hebrew word for "sees" there is "blepo" (Strongs Greek #991), and it means "to look at, to see, to perceive and to discern." HELPS Word-studies further indicates that the word suggests, *"to see something physical, with spiritual results. That is, it carries what is seen into the non-physical (immaterial) realm so a person can take the needed action."* (6)

Let's come before the Lord in that posture of prayer today.

God, would you *help me to remember*, that You are *IN the Secret*. If I want to find you, I can go there. And I don't need my interactions and encounters withyou, to be anything that anyone else would ever see or notice.

Knowing that You see me in the Secret, is enough for me today.

When I am tempted to walk the wrong path, cross-examine and test me, and guide me in the way I should go...back to the Secret and the Sacred.

Jesus, I come before you in honest prayer and confession. Is there anything that I need to unlearn and relearn, or *remember again* today about Your Word, and Your heart for me?"

Day 7 / Rest

When I remember, rightly, who You already are, Jesus, I can truly find rest in You, even if it is deep within the Secret, and the Sacred.

Lord, when I think about Your heart, and I remember that above all else, You are after my heart, I am prompted to position myself to truly encounter who You are. My heart is to enjoy You, to worship You, to learn from You, and to bring You glory, Jesus.

Bring to my remembrance, what I have read and studied in Your Word. Help me to remember that I can separate myself from the desire to be seen and known by others, for the way I love, serve and follow You. Examine my heart, Lord, and if the lines ever get blurry on who is actually receiving the glory from letting my light so shine for You, would you show me that?

I am reminded again today, that so many of Your words, Jesus, use a *present and ongoing tense* in their grammar, which reminds me that You'd know I would need these deep *truths over and over,* again. I can tell by the words that You use, that You knew I would not just learn these things once, and then remember them for life. Knowing my heart like only You do, You gave me the Holy Spirit to bring to my remembrance the things You'd already taught me but knew I might forget. Jesus, I know it is not a surprise to You when I forget, but I rest in knowing that it is Your lovingkindness that draws me into repentance. Teach me and bring to my remembrance all that You've already taught me to be true. Remind me again, of the beauty that is seen only in the Secret and the Sacred, Lord.

Teach my heart to long for, celebrate and value what happens in the Secret, alone withyou. Even if no one else ever knows, and even if I never speak another word about what You let me be a part of, Lord, help me to celebrate those moments, even still.

Remind me that *other people knowing about those encounters is not what makes them special and valuable. I too, can go and tell no one.*

And I can Remember and Rest, in knowing that You Jesus, love, and value what happens in the Secret and the Sacred. Help me to remember that there is a difference in doing something *for You*, and something *withyou*, in Secret.

Jesus, today I want to remember who You are, and what I already know to be true of You. Today I remember that Your Word tells me...

When I stop and remember, I can rest in who You already are, and what You have already done.

When I know and remember...

I can rest in...

Jesus, in light of what I have learned this week, and as I position my heart to remember and rest, this is the prayer of my heart....

Week 5

Day 1

Last week in Matthew 6, we saw Jesus warning against public displays of righteousness that might have their roots in a desire to be noticed, valued and applauded by others. We saw Jesus giving instructions to instead, seek the Father, *in secret*. When we take a step back and look closely at Matthew 6, as well as all of the "go and tell no one" passages that we've studied, we see that Jesus clearly desires for the posture of our hearts to be turned toward Him, and what He is doing both in us, and our personal stories, as well as what He is doing in the Kingdom. We've established that we don't always get to see or understand the fullness of what He is doing in the big picture, and sometimes He is just calling us to trust Him, in the Secret Places. In the "go and tell no one" passages, Jesus is forever changing the lives of those that He encounters, but His instructions are to "tell no one." We know the reason for that was partly due to the way He wanted His ministry to unfold, and for people to not just observe and be impressed by what He could do, but also, that they would come to know and understand WHO He was, as well. We can identify with that tendency… to be drawn to the public side, and the displays and works of Jesus, and gravitating towards the big and exciting and visible parts that come along with following Him. We can be guilty of that too, in our day and in our generation, valuing more what we get to say about Him or things we get to go to or be a part of, more than secret encounters of Jesus we have that no one will ever know about.

The interesting thing is, that by looking at Scripture, we see that Jesus valued those secret and sacred moments. Both in the interactions He had with people, when He said, "go and don't tell anyone about this," as well as the way that He lived His own life, interacting with the Father.

Even in His own life, we see that some seasons in the life of Jesus were seasons of reaping and of harvest, visible and lived out in front of others to see. And even in the very life of Jesus, some seasons were appointed as seasons of sowing, lived out in the hiddenness of a quiet life, being shaped and prepared to tend to the business of the Father. Think about how much we know about Jesus that comes from His season of public ministry… But think also about how much of that season was shaped in the quietness of the thirty or so years that we know very little about. We can see that the Father assigns value and purpose in what happens in the Secret and the Sacred. It helps us to reframe what we think about the Secret and the Sacred…it's not that those moments are overlooked or unnoticed…it's just that they serve a different purpose, and God is brought glory in a different way. Even in the life and ministry of Jesus, these encounters continue to have value and worth assigned to them, *even if they are never spoken about again*. We can hold onto that same truth in our own lives. Jesus encourages us to seek the Father, in secret, in the everyday moments of our daily lives, and to remember that He not only sees us in secret but that He values what happens there.

Today, we are going to look at what Jesus says about the rewards that are found in the Secret, and ask Him to help us remember again, what it means to treasure the right treasure.

Let's begin today by remembering Jesus in the "go and tell no one" passages, and also returning to our study of Matthew 6 from last week.

Let's read Matthew 6 again, but looking at it with fresh eyes today, and making special note of what Jesus says about "reward."

Matthew 6 (NASB)

6 "Beware of practicing your righteousness before men to be noticed by them; otherwise you have no *reward* with your Father who is in heaven. 2 "So when you give to the poor, do not sound a trumpet before you, as the hypocrites do in the synagogues and in the streets, so that they may be honored by men. Truly I say to you, they have their reward in full. 3 But when you give to the poor, do not let your left hand know what your right hand is doing, 4 so that your giving will be in secret; and your Father who sees what is done in secret will *reward* you. 5 "When you pray, you are not to be like the hypocrites; for they love to stand and pray in the synagogues and on the street corners so that they may be seen by men. Truly I say to you, they have their reward in full. 6 But you, when you pray, go into your inner room, close your door and pray to your Father who is in secret, and your Father who sees what is done in secret will *reward* you. 7 "And when you are praying, do not use meaningless repetition as the Gentiles do, for they suppose that they will be heard for their many words. 8 So do not be like them; for your Father knows what you need before you ask Him."

Make observations and write down each time that Jesus says "*reward.*"

Just by looking at this passage alone, what is Jesus stirring up in you already, today?

Day 2

Let's ask God to open our eyes to see all the treasures that He has for us in this passage, as we look a little deeper at what the original language says here.

Use an Interlinear Bible, or Strong's Exhaustive Concordance of the Bible to look up the Greek word for "reward" that Jesus uses in this passage in Matthew 6. (Again, you can literally type this in your search window, and research this online, if you don't have access to physical copies of these tools.) Make notes about what you discover here…

The English word "reward" used in Matthew 6 is translated to the Greek word _____, which is Strong's # _____.
The definition is:

Hopefully, if that is a new practice for you, you tried it on your own. If you'd like to do that together, you can peek here. The definition we get from Strong's Concordance for "reward" in Matthew 6:1 is the Greek word, "misthos," which is a masculine noun meaning "wages, salary, reward." The HELPS Word-study further explains that it is essentially, a reward that appropriately compensates a particular decision or action. (1)

Look again, at each time the word "reward" is mentioned.

The context that Jesus is speaking into here, is a familiar one…the condition of the heart. Jesus literally says, "beware," as He speaks against those whose motives are so "that they may be honored by men." That phrase Jesus uses in Matthew 6, verse 2 is described in the Greek from the word "doxazo," Strongs #1392 which is a verb meaning "to render or esteem glorious." (Look it up if you're interested!) It indicates the action of glorifying, honoring, bestowing glory on, ascribing weight or value to something or someone. (2)

What does Jesus say about that type of reward, in Matthew 6:1?

In the Sermon on the Mount, Jesus is giving us instructions for what it looks like to follow Him, and He continues to give shape to what He means when He calls something "blessed" (which He does MANY times, in the Sermon on the Mount). The words He uses help us to understand what it means to be characterized by the quality of God and to be fully satisfied by the indwelling of Christ, not by circumstances.

Jesus guards against the motive of working for the approval of others, and says that yields "no reward with your Father in heaven." Instead, He encourages us to seek the Lord, "in secret," by our actions, and in our spirit. He then distinguishes the difference in the reward that comes with being seen and noticed by and the "reward" given by our Father who sees in secret. Two different verbs are used there to describe the nature of being given these two different types of rewards. Using an Interlinear Bible, or Strong's, do some research on the definition of the word Jesus uses to describe how the Father, who sees in secret "will reward" or "repay" you, in Matthew 6:4, 6:6, and 6:18. Write down your observations.

The Greek word there, "apodidomi," Strongs #591 is a verb meaning "to give back, return, restore, render as due." (3) So, the reward of being noticed by others is "paid in full," when someone notices you doing something righteous.

But the reward for righteous actions towards God done in secret, are rewarded or repaid, in kind, by the Father who is in secret and sees in secret. What do you imagine that type of reward to be?

In closing today, let's read on in Matthew 6:19-21, where Jesus gives more instructions about that type of reward.

Matthew 6:19-21 (NASB)
19 "Do not store up for yourselves treasures on earth, where moth and rust destroy, and where thieves break in and steal. 20 But store up for yourselves treasures in heaven, where neither moth nor rust destroys, and where thieves do not break in or steal; 21 for where your treasure is, there your heart will be also."

Take note of what Jesus says about "treasure," and write down your thoughts here...

Day 3

We've been looking at what Jesus has to say in Matthew 6 about "treasures" and being rewarded from "the Father in secret."

Do a word study of the word "treasure" in **Matthew 6:19-21**. Write down any observations and thoughts here…

If you looked at the original Greek word for treasure, "thesaurus," Strongs #2344, you probably made note of its description as a masculine noun, meaning "*a treasure, or a store,*" "*a storehouse for precious things.*" The HELPS word-study, tells us that the word comes from the verb, "tithemi" meaning "*to put, set,*" indicating "*stored up treasure, riches,*" and figuratively, a "*storehouse of treasure, including treasured thoughts stored up in the heart and mind.*" Incidentally, *thēsaurós* is the root of the English term "*thesaurus*" which refers to a "storehouse (treasure) of synonyms," and *thēsaurós* is literally "a receptacle for valuables." (4)

In light of these insights from the original language, read Matthew 6:1-21 again, and write down any new thoughts or observations here…

Think about your own experience with the two different types of rewards (or treasures), that Jesus describes throughout Matthew 6. Think about your own life, and your own experience and write down some moments in your story that you've encountered what Jesus is speaking about here…

Does talking about this kind of treasure, make you think about a really, really familiar part of Scripture when we see someone else "treasuring" something in this way?

Read the familiar passage in **Luke 2**, that we read each year at Christmas. Write out the words you find in verse 19, and write out any observations or insights, specifically in that passage...

This may very well be a familiar passage of Scripture to you, and if so, consider looking at this passage about Mary with fresh eyes today. Do a word study on the Greek word for "treasure" in Luke 2:19 and write any thoughts or observations down here...

We already have so many reasons to be endeared to Mary, mother of Jesus, but even more so when we read about her here. The word used to describe what Mary did, when she "treasured up all these things, pondering them in her heart," is Strong's Greek word #4933, which is *"suntereo,"* meaning *"to keep close, to preserve."* The HELPS Word-study indicates that it means *"to guard, to keep, to preserve close together, with close care, to keep intact and safe."* (5)

How does what Mary did, when she "treasured up all these things, pondering them in her heart" compare to the two different types of "rewards" or "treasures," that her own Son, Jesus, would speak about years later in Matthew 6?

How do these words about Mary inspire you today? If there was ever a time that someone had great cause to "go public," and "be noticed and be seen by others," we'd certainly think that the birth of the Messiah would qualify. And yet, we see Mary doing the opposite. We see Mary modeling what it would look like to interact with the Father, who sees in secret and rewards in secret, and after a life-changing encounter with Him, choose to *"treasure up all these things,"* by *"preserving them, guarding them, keeping them close and safe."* What is Jesus, Himself stirring up in you as you think on this?

Day 4

Of course, tucked in a passage of Scripture that we return to every year, and could maybe even say, by heart, is a beautiful, life-changing bit of truth. *Of course*, the Father who sees in secret, and rewards in secret, would set deep in the heart of Mary, a desire "to treasure" and to pre-serve, and keep close the intimacy, the beauty, the wonder, and the life-changing gift of Heaven come to earth. *Of course*, the baby, who'd come to change the world, would not come to live among us with sounds of trumpets, and fanfare, but in the choosing of the secret, hidden, inti-mate, and ordinary quietness of the manger. And *of course*, this baby, who had come to tell us the good news of the upside-down kingdom of God, was wrapped in swaddling clothes, and held close to His mother, as she held close in the Secret Places of her heart, what God had done.

We learn a lot about Mary when we read these words, but we also learn a lot about Jesus, when we look at how He chose to come be Immanuel, God with us.

Thayer's Greek Lexicon describes Mary's "treasuring" with the definition, "to keep within oneself," and Strong's Exhaustive Concordance says that "by implication, it is to conserve, to remember and obey." And even the original Greek word used for the word, "pondered" in verse 19, implies to "*bring together in one's mind, to confer with oneself.*" (6)

Here Mary lets us peek in, and reframes for us, what it would look like to treasure the right treasure. She had the most intimate, extraordinary encounter with God, and yet her instinct was to keep it close, and sacred, rather than make it known to all. God had set in her heart, this idea of the Secret and the Sacred, and she knew to treasure it. The baby she held in her arms would one day grow up and astound the world with a gospel that was far from the one they ex-pected. Part of the great redemption story of Jesus was that *through Him*, and the true posture of our heart toward Him, we could be made right with God. What is hidden in the Secret Places of our own heart, can be seen by the Father who is *in secret*, and *sees in secret*.

Once again, this thread is actually even woven into the story of the life of Jesus, isn't it? While His name and His renown have become the treasure of Christians throughout the cen-turies, the majority of His very own life was lived out in hidden and unseen places. We don't have a detailed picture of the first *thirty years* of His life, reminding us of the beauty of seasons, and how God is always working in the larger story.

Jesus spent much of His ministry giving value to what is done for the Father, in secret. And just like we've seen over and over again, He gave value to a personal encounter He'd had with someone in secret, even urging them not to speak of it, again.

In light of the insights from Matthew 6, as well as Luke 2, let's take some time to identify some of the differences we've seen.

In Matthew 6, Jesus spoke about rewards that come with being "seen" or "noticed" by others.

Make a list of some of the "treasures" or "rewards" that come in ways that other people *can see?*

Now, make a list of "treasures" or "rewards" that come in ways that *no one else would see.*

Again, when we see Jesus speaking about this, He is after the deepest, most intimate parts of our hearts. He sees it (even if we don't say it out loud, or see it ourselves), and He encourages us to lift our eyes to see beyond what is right in front of us, and to instead, treasure the Secret and the Sacred, even if it remains hidden and unknown to others. When we reflect back on Mary and the birth of Christ, it is easy to see now, that these events would be talked about every year, for thousands of years, and would change mankind forever. And yet Scripture paints a picture for us of something that looked less like a huge, worldwide event, and more like a secret and sacred moment when Mary got to see heaven come to earth and the miraculous break into the ordinary. Mary got to see the promises that she'd heard her whole life come true, and she saw them unfolding inside her, and in front of her, in miraculous ways. And yet again, we see her choosing to preserve those sacred moments, by keeping them close within her own heart.

What is God stirring up in you today, to treasure and ponder, that no one else may ever see or know or talk about?

Day 5

We continue to see in Scripture, that in the most amazing, miraculous, and life-changing moments, God's heart for us is not always, to share or proclaim it, but sometimes, *instead to keep it close, preserve it and tell no one.*

How does that strike you today, in light of what you continue to read and study?

What do you think compels a person, to grow to have the heart of Mary, and to instinctively determine when an encounter is something to be treasured and preserved in the Secret and the Sacred?

Like most things, the ways of the world are almost opposite of the ways of Christ. We'll never be able to look at the world, and all that it tells us, and somehow, accidentally end up with a heart after God's own heart.

The upside-down Kingdom of Jesus can only be seen and understood, in light of His Word, and with a Holy Spirit revealed knowledge, therein.

Learning how to treasure the right treasure comes in spending time with Jesus, and learning what He, Himself treasures. And the instinct to identify a moment that is best preserved in the Secret, and the Sacred, comes with knowing the heart of Jesus and turning our own hearts there.

Let's look at what God's Word has to say about having the mind of Christ, and turning our heart towards a more eternal perspective and Kingdom mindset.

Read these passages, and make notes of any observations you have.

Romans 12:2 (NASB)
And do not be conformed to this world, but be transformed by the renewing of your mind, so that you may prove what the will of God is, that which is good and acceptable and perfect.

Philippians 4:8-9 (NIV)
8 Finally, brothers and sisters, whatever is true, whatever is noble, whatever is right, whatever is pure, whatever is lovely, whatever is admirable—if anything is excellent or praiseworthy—think about such things. 9 Whatever you have learned or received or heard from me, or seen in me—put it into practice. And the God of peace will be withyou.

2 Corinthians 4:16-18 (NASB)
16 Therefore we do not lose heart, but though our outer man is decaying, yet our inner man is being renewed day by day. 17 For momentary, light affliction is producing for us an eternal weight of glory far beyond all comparison, 18 while we look not at the things which are seen, but at the things which are not seen; for the things which are seen are temporal, but the things which are not seen are eternal.

In studying these passages, in light of the "go and tell no one" encounters, as well as the words of Jesus in Matthew 6, and then looking at the way "Mary treasured up all these things and pondered them in her heart, we are given an important opportunity to reflect. The Bible has much to say about what is "seen" and "known," and talks a lot about the unseen, and what is hidden, and in "the Secret," as well. In fact, the encouragement of 2 Corinthians 4: 18 above, in one translation says, *"we fix our gaze on things that cannot be seen."*

I think most of us have had plenty of practice seeing what the world sees, and giving value to what is seen and noticed by others.

What would it look like to see, and give value to, things known only in the Secret and the Sacred? Pray and reflect, and write your thoughts here.

Day 6/ Remember

Isaiah 45:3 (NIV)
I will give you hidden treasures, riches stored in se-
cret places, so that you may know that I am the LORD,
the God of Israel, who summons you by name.

It is a profound privilege when Jesus entrusts us with a Secret and Sacred moment when heaven comes to earth, and no one will ever even know or speak of it again. What a gift it is when Jesus invites us into secret and sacred moments, and we feel the pleasure of being *let in* on something profoundly beautiful, *just between us.* Those moments are to be treasured, and given value because Jesus values them. Moments that happen in the unseen are not given value only if they *become seen.* Sometimes the treasure of knowing and following Jesus is found in the Secret and the Sacred, not in the public or the visible. Jesus speaks about treasure that is in the Secret and in the unseen, and also encourages us to seek the Father, who is in secret. *When we remember that the true treasure is Jesus and that an encounter with Him is a reward, even if unseen, we honor His heart for us.* Positioning our hearts to remember this, helps us to reframe what our hearts treasure. Our hearts learn to treasure the right treasure, and we remember that things that are seen, or shared are not more valuable than things that are unseen, secret and sacred. What might that look like in our own sacred relationship with Jesus today?

If you are on Social Media, then you have undoubtedly come across the phenomenon, that is "Instagram Best 9!" In short, an app uses an algorithm to determine which of your 9 photos from the last year received the most "likes" from friends on Instagram. It creates a collage of those 9 posts, and at the end of the year, (the last few years, anyway), all of our Instagram feeds have been filled with these collages. (You might have even done one yourself!) Instagram Best 9 identifies which posts, seen by those around us, most resonated with those following us.

What if we used that same concept, but began to give value to things that were sacred and unseen, hidden from anyone else? Scripture continues to compel us to look for the reward given in secret, and to fix our eyes on the unseen, and to treasure what Jesus treasures. *What if we actually did that!?* What if we took on the heart of Mary and valued the Secret and Sacred and holy moments in our lives, and we preserved them and valued them by keeping them close, remembering them, treasuring them…honoring them in the quietness of our heart?

The Old Testament tells us about how the prophet Samuel set up a stone and called it "Ebenezer," to be a physical reminder of the powerful way God had shown His goodness, and faithfulness to the people of Israel after He led them to a victory over the Philistines. After a season of repentance and seeking the LORD, the Israelites, began to see this stone as *a way to remember*. Whenever the Israelites would pass by the stone, they would remember how the LORD had acted on their behalf.

We, like people of Israel, often need help to remember the ways that God works in our lives, especially in ways we cannot see. Maybe, we too need an Ebenezer? Something physical, that we can touch and hold, to remind us of the spiritual truth, that God sees us, in the Secret and the Sacred?

What if we made our own secret Ebenezer to remember the significant moments when God lets us in on the Secret and the Sacred, right in the middle of our everyday? An Ebenezer for the Secret and Sacred could be a list, hidden away in a journal, or pieces of paper recalling sacred encounters with Jesus, tucked away in a jar, or a box, that no one else knows about.

Spend some time today, asking the Holy Spirit to bring to your remembrance, times that you've shared in the Secret and the Sacred, in the unseen moments where God is moving, and He let you be a part of them. Ask Him to teach you to *see* those moments, *value* them and *celebrate* them. Think about making an Ebenezer, whether written down physically or just written in your heart. Remember those moments… celebrate them. Like Mary, ponder those moments, treasure them, and hold them close, as you remember. And then, *go and tell no one about it.*

After reading and studying this week, I remember again, that despite all the treasures this world has to offer, You, God are the treasure I seek.

What I most feel you stirring up in me is…

Day 7/ Rest

Lord, we begin today by setting our hearts at rest and thinking on Your Word.

Colossians 2:2-4 (MSG)

2-4 I want you woven into a tapestry of love, in touch with everything there is to know of God. Then you will have minds confident and *at rest*, focused on Christ, God's great mystery. All the richest treasures of wisdom and knowledge are embedded in that mystery and nowhere else.

Lord, when I read these words from Scripture, I remember again that You tell me that all the richest treasures are hidden in the Secret withyou. What I feel You stirring up in me is this...

Lord, this is my prayer for encountering You, in the Secret and the Sacred...

Lord, when I remember all that Your Word revealed to me this week, I remember again that *You are the treasure*. This world has nothing to offer me that can compare to knowing You, and encountering You in the Secret and the Sacred Places. Help me to remember again, that there is a difference in doing something *for You*, and something *withyou*, in Secret. I rest in knowing that when I am in the Secret Places withyou, and I get to enjoy Sacred moments that you invite me to be a part of, that no one will ever know about, that you have led me to walk on Holy Ground. I will treasure You, and those Secret and Sacred moments withyou, above all else.

Today, I choose to remember and rest in Your Word. I will fix my eyes again on the riches of your Word, and remember again, where my true treasure lies.

Rest in God alone, my soul,
for my hope comes from him.
Psalm 62:5 (CSB)

When I remember…

I rest in…

Today, Lord, I want to Remember and Rest in the Secret and the Sacred, and this is the prayer of my heart…

My son, if you receive my words
and treasure up my commandments withyou,
making your ear attentive to wisdom
and inclining your heart to understanding;
yes, if you call out for insight
and raise your voice for understanding,
if you seek it like silver
and search for it as for hidden treasures,
then you will understand the fear of the Lord
and find the knowledge of God.
For the Lord gives wisdom;
from his mouth come knowledge and understanding;

Proverbs 2:1-6

Week 6

Day 1

He who dwells in the Secret Place of the Most High
will rest in the shadow of the Almighty.
Psalm 91:1 (WEB)

Where can we find rest?

Psalm 91 tells us that those who *dwell in the Secret Place will find rest.* In your own words, write your first impressions of this verse.

It's interesting where this journey has taken us, isn't it?

We started by looking at some of the more unfamiliar words of Jesus in the "go and tell no one" encounters found in the gospels. In seeking to understand those words of Jesus, we found that He is often working in ways we can't see, and we often don't have the whole picture of His Kingdom purposes. We may have even seen ourselves in the crowds of people, wanting to get close to Jesus because of what He could do for them, instead of worshiping Him for who He really was. We watched as time and time again, Jesus stepped right into a life-changing encounter with someone, but only after calling them away from the eyes of the crowd and into a more private and intimate setting, already seeing deep inside their hearts. We have come to know the heart of Jesus for all who encounter Him to truly understand Him and to be able to hear His gospel of grace and freedom. We've come to understand the call to follow Him because of His great and saving love for us, not just His ability to meet our needs. We have heard His words as He warns against the desire to be noticed and applauded and acclaimed by man, but to instead seek the Father in secret. We have uncovered what God's Word already says that true reward really is, and what it might look like in our own lives, to treasure the right treasure. And so today, as we near the end of our journey together, we'll yet again ask the Lord to open our eyes to the wonders in His Word, as week seek to have a soul at rest.

I love the way that God's Word is so trustworthy, and passages in the Old Testament echo truths, and promises and wisdom in the New Testament, and vice versa. All of the words of Jesus that encourage us to seek the Father in secret are magnified and validated in the words of the Psalmist that had already been set apart for generations... *"He who dwells in the Secret Place of the Most High will rest in the shadow of the Almighty..."*

Where do we find rest? We find it when we dwell in the Secret Place with Him. The answer to one of those questions of the ages... "what will bring this soul of mine rest?"

God's Word points us to an answer found hidden in the Secret and the Sacred.

Maybe you've been living with the same heart posture that the people of Israel had adopted for as long as anyone could remember...that the way you get to God depends on what you *do for Him.* That at the end of the day, the devotion and righteousness displayed, would be measured and totaled, in an effort to reach a Holy God.

Here we see the words of Jesus, being echoed by God's heart for us that had been there all along. *It's not in the doing that we find rest...it's in the being.*

And it's not in the ways that we publicly display our devotion, but rather *our heart for the Father, found in the Secret.*

Depending on what Bible translation you use, you might read Psalm 91:1 with these words:

"The one who lives under the protection of the Most High dwells in the shadow of the Almighty."

Or

"He who dwells in the shelter of the Most High will abide in the shadow of the Almighty."

Our English translations may use a few different words to paint this picture for us, but the roots of the Hebrew words are clear. Look at an Interlinear Bible translation, or your favorite way to study words in the original language, and write your observations about the keywords in Psalm 91:1.

What is Christ stirring up in you today, as you seek wisdom from His Word about "rest?"

Day 2

If you did some research yesterday, your word study may have shed new light on what God's Word says about the Secret Place. The Hebrew words used in Psalm 91 paint a picture of the Secret place being "a covering, a shelter, a hiding place, and a place of protection." (1)

There is another place in Scripture that we often hear being associated with those types of words. Do you remember that encounter that Moses has with God in Exodus 33, at the tent of meeting? I've mentioned before that the name of our ministry "Withyou," is actually inspired by the words that God speaks to Moses over, and over again throughout Exodus, promising, "I will be withyou." Just like in Exodus 3, when God first called Moses from the burning bush, to lead His people to freedom, we see Him promising that again in Exodus 33. It says, "the LORD used to speak to Moses face to face, just as a man speaks to his friend." In Exodus 33:14, God says to Moses, "My *presence will go with you, and I will give you rest.*" What our English translations don't clearly say for us, is what the Hebrew translation offers there. When it says, "I will give you rest," the form of the conjugated verb there implies, it is "*usually followed by a person.*" (2) God's action of bringing us rest, is closely tied to *Him being with us....literally. It is in God's "with-ness" that we find rest.* After once again, promising to be with Him, just a few sentences later in Exodus 33, is where we see God physically hiding Moses in the cleft of a rock, offering a covering in the secret, while also fulfilling His promise that His presence would be with Him.

God continues to draw us near to Him, offering rest, that comes along with being in the Secret Place. Let's read the words in the first verse of Psalm 91 again.

"He who dwells in the Secret Place of the Most High will rest in the shadow of the Almighty."

To further solidify this Biblical truth in our hearts, let's look at it another way. Think of seeing a shadow. A shadow is cast when something tangible and physical stands in the path of the sun's rays, right? The invisible, imperceptible, "thought" of something or the "concept" of something wouldn't cast a shadow, would it? Something real and tangible and physically present is what casts a shadow. So, when we read here that, "he who dwells in the Secret Place of the Most High will rest in the shadow of the Almighty," it isn't implying that, *in theory.* The choice of words used here... "*resting in the shadow* of the Almighty," implies that *a shadow is cast because He is physically there in that Secret Place with us.* This is not an empty promise made, in theory.

When God says, "*My presence will go withyou, and I will give you rest,*" He means, "My presence will *literally be withyou.*" God brings rest to us, when we are in the Secret Place with Him. *And He is there with us.*

And the concept here is not that "the Secret Place" with Him is a place we go to from time to time, to check back in. The words here say, *"He who dwells."*

Do a word study on the original Hebrew word used in Psalm 91:1 for "dwells" at the beginning of the phrase in English. Write your observations and insights here…

If you searched online or used an Interlinear Bible or Strong's Exhaustive Concordance of the Bible, you probably noted that "He who dwells" in the Hebrew, comes from the verb, "yashab" (Strongs #3427), which means "to sit, remain, dwell." The implication is that one who "dwells" in this designated place, remains there, *in an ongoing sense*, and becomes "an inhabitant" there. (3) This is not a come and go, visit periodically, type of thing. It is a "this is my home…this is where I live," kind of thing. Further reinforcing this, is the phrase at the end of Psalm 91:1 for "will rest," which is often translated "will abide."

What is Christ stirring up in you, as you begin to think about resting in the Secret Place, with these new insights?

Psalm 91 paints a picture for us, that rest is closely connected to the Secret place. What would it look like to live, from a place of rest, believing God is always withyou, and that your home is abiding in the Secret place with Him?

Let's close by reading the words of **Psalm 27:4-6.**

> **4 I have asked one thing from the Lord. This I will seek: to remain in the Lord's house all the days of my life in order to gaze at the Lord's beauty and to search for an answer in His temple. 5 He hides me in His shelter when there is trouble. He keeps me hidden in His tent. He sets me high on a rock. 6 Now my head will be raised above my enemies who surround me. I will offer sacrifices with shouts of joy in His tent. I will sing and make music to praise the Lord.**

Day 3

Read the words of Jesus to the disciples in Mark 6:31.

Mark 6:31
"Let's go off by ourselves to a quiet place and rest awhile..."

What do you think of when you hear the word "rest?"

What do you think Jesus meant when He used the word "rest" in Mark 6:31?

Jesus gave some suggestions about where this rest could happen, and what it could look like. What does that mean to you today?

It is important for us to identify what Scripture means and exactly what it is implied, when that particular word, "rest," is used. Because here's the thing....

It's easy to talk about a word like "rest" when we find ourselves in a beautiful place, or we are able to slow down, and de-stress and relax a bit. When we wake up in the morning, and our view is the sun rising over the horizon, shining onto a sandy beach, or a majestic mountain, or a picturesque lake, we can't help but start to breathe a little more deeply.

The real challenge is in believing that same rest is available to us, right in the middle of our everyday lives. We don't have to go on vacation to find rest. The rest we long for isn't limited to the number of personal days we get per year. It's not just a "siesta," lay in the sun with your toes in the sand, kind of rest...although that is lovely and certainly a gift. A lazy morning sleeping in, laying on a hammock, or for some, a round of golf or a long bike ride, are all amazing ways to settle our minds and our bodies, for sure. But we'll find ourselves quickly restless again if we think that is what will finally bring rest to our souls.

Think back to what we learned yesterday from Psalm 91 when we studied the original Hebrew word used in the phrase, "he who dwells." The Hebrew word there implies that "one who dwells in the Secret Place" will find rest, in an *ongoing* sense, because it is the place where they live. Some versions phrase it "will rest," and some phrase it "will abide," but both imply that this is an ongoing action...and from this, is where the rest, the covering, the with-ness of God is. It is not a go, and get filled up, and then try to go back to our lives, kind of rest.

What Jesus offers to us every single moment of every single day, right in the middle of our everyday lives, is a settled, soul-rest. It is ours in the Secret place with Him. We find it in the practice of stopping to remember who He says that He is, and who He says that we are, in Him.

That rest is ours when we remember to preach to our own souls, what He has ALREADY done, and that He promises to be with us, always. These are the truths that we so often forget to remember.

The confession of St. Augustine, just a few hundred years after Christ, is the same confession of our hearts today, whether we can articulate it or not...

> "You have made us for yourself,
> O Lord, and our heart is restless until it rests in you."

It is not what we see with our eyes that bring us rest. It's not the absence of responsibilities or stress that bring us rest. It's not the sound of the crashing waves, or the sand in our toes, that brings rest. It's not a healthy family, a safe home, or a steady paycheck, that brings rest. A comfortable life, without tension or worry, is not even the thing that will ultimately bring us rest. And being able to live a life with passion and purpose, or being known as someone who is making a mark on the world, are not the things that will stop the aching in our souls.

What each of those things offers *is relief*. And relief is good. Relief can make it easier to catch our breath. But *relief is not rest*.

And having a temporary sense of relief wasn't ever meant to satisfy the deepest longings of our hearts.

When we think that a certain set of circumstances, whatever we imagine those to be, will bring us lasting peace and rest, we miss the deep, abiding rest that comes only in Jesus…only in the Secret Place with Him. When we remember what we already know to be true, only then, can we find the rest we so desperately long for…

Despite what is happening around us, *deep soul-rest is already in us, and it's ours in Christ when we choose to remember and abide with Him in the Secret Place.* Jesus is offering it today… right there in your kitchen, in your cubicle, in your car, or on your couch.

Ask the Lord to open your eyes to what it could look like to live from a place of rest, abiding in the Secret place, believing He is there withyou, in your own life, today. Write your thoughts here…

Day 4

We've spent the last six weeks together reading the "go and tell no one" passages, and studying the words of Jesus about the Secret and the Sacred.

In reading God's Word, we have seen how Jesus often drew people into a secret and sacred encounter, away from the eyes of the crowd. We saw Him graciously interacting and responding to the countless people who flocked to Him with an inadequate picture of who He really was, and what He could really bring to their lives. In studying the Sermon on the Mount, in Matthew 5 and 6, we saw Jesus guarding against a life of faith, lived out in public with a desire to be seen, or noticed or even applauded by others. So many times we saw Jesus valuing intimacy with Him, even if unseen by others, and encouraged us to take on the attitude of seeking the Father in Secret, and looking for our treasure there. We were inspired by the heart of Mary, the beloved Mother of Jesus, and how during one of the most epic, world-changing moments the world would ever know, she "pondered these things and treasured them in her heart." We were reminded again, that Jesus is the true reward, and all the richest treasures of wisdom and knowledge are in the mystery of the Secret Place with Him. We have seen and remembered again, that our souls find rest when we continue to dwell in the Secret Place of the Most High.

It has been said that *"every feeling we have is rooted in a belief."* As followers of Jesus, it is crucial to investigate if the beliefs we have are rooted in His Truth, from His Word, or from somewhere else.

Did any of the passages we've read over the last weeks challenge a feeling you often have? And if so, did it challenge a belief, you may not have even known you had?

Because Jesus knew our hearts so well, and the range of fleeting emotions that come with being human, He spoke right into our soul's need to *abide* in Him. Our study of Psalm 91 on Day 1 of this week, reminds us that rest follows *dwelling*, or *abiding*, with God in the Secret Place. We remember again that the call to dwell or abide, is *ongoing* and *continuous*… not something we fill up on once and then have to go back to again to get more when we run out. (4) It can be easy to think about that rest that comes from dwelling and abiding in the Secret Place, as something that happens only on one day of the week, or just at certain points of our day. We can mistakenly think that it's a place we go visit….as if, we'd enter into that place of rest, and then pack it all up in our suitcase and then take it back to place where we live our real lives. God's Word, instead, points over and over again, to an *ongoing, abiding, and continuous* dwelling in the Secret Place with Jesus, is what brings rest. Living *from* that posture of continuously dwelling, or abiding, in Jesus, alone is the only thing that can bring our hearts true rest.

When each of us remembers that our deepest longing is for Jesus alone and that our home is a continuous abiding, and dwelling in the Secret Place with Him, then we can always find rest. And that rest is not affected by circumstances. The feelings and emotions that occasionally stir up in us, because of our circumstances, do not take away that rest. We may need to remember what we already know to be true when circumstances tempt us to forget. But the truth is, our rest is secure when we stay in the posture of continuously abiding in the Secret Place with Jesus. No matter what emotions stir up in us in that moment. Whether we are feeling misunderstood, alone, unappreciated, looked over, inadequate, or small, or whether we are on the other end of the spectrum feeling known, pursued, understood, appreciated, validated, and secure…

The rest Jesus offers is not dependent on those things, so it is continuously ours, in the Secret Place with Him.

Over, 100 times in God's Word, from Genesis to Revelation, God promises, "I will be withyou." We've read several times how, in Exodus, He says it this way… "My presence will go withyou, and I will give you rest."

The root of believing that promise that God is withyou, is what leads to the path of a life, abiding in Him, in the Secret and the Sacred. Think about it…

If I believe that He is always with me, then that means that *He is already there with me in the Secret and the Sacred.*

He knows. He sees.

He invites me to share in that with Him.
I don't even need to say another word.

I can rest *with* Him in those silent, secret and sacred moments.

The way that I follow Jesus and help to build His Kingdom right here in my own community, in my own home, in my own family are all lived out, *together with Jesus*, in the Secret and Sacred, *even if I go and tell no one.*

Think about your journey over the last six weeks and write out the words of one of the passages that God used most to stir up your heart.

Put into your own words how you feel God stirring you to remember and rest, because of that passage.

Day 5
So, is it "Go and Tell," or "Go and Tell No One?"

That's a good question, isn't it? What do you think? Is the command, "go and tell," or is the command, "go and tell no one?"

That may have been an unfair question, because if you answered "both," then you're right. There are multiple times in Scripture that encouragement is given to both, "*go and tell,*" as well as, "*go and tell no one.*" The difference, of course, has to do with the situation, as well as the condition of our hearts.

When we look back at the context of many of the "go and tell no one" passages, there is a caution on the part of Jesus, that He is not introduced or paraded around, as the long-awaited Messiah, without the context of His teaching about the good news of the gospel. We have probably all been witness to the words or the blessings of Jesus, being used out of context. Like we talked about way back in Week 1, Jesus loves us too much, to limit our relationship with Him, to simple transactions that are only about getting our needs met, and our requests answered. Jesus has offered Himself, and a relationship with Him, as Lord of our lives, as a way to be restored to the Father. He longs for a relationship with us, where we position Him as the Savior and Lord of our lives, and from that place of protection, obedience, and rest, we walk in His freedom and grace and truth.

Philippians 2 reminds us how Christ Jesus, although He existed in the form of God, emptied Himself, taking on the form of a bondservant, and was made in the likeness of man. The words in the gospel of **John 1:10-14**, paint a beautiful picture for us.

> **10 He was in the world, and the world was made through Him, and
> the world did not know Him. 11 He came to His own, and those
> who were His own did not receive Him. 12 But as many as received
> Him, to them He gave the right to become children of God, even
> to those who believe in His name, 13 who were born, not of blood
> nor of the will of the flesh nor of the will of man, but of God.
> 14 And the Word became flesh, and dwelt among us, and we saw
> His glory, glory as of the only begotten from the Father,
> full of grace and truth.**

Jesus became *Immanuel, God with us.* He lived and dwelt among us. He came to be *with* us, to get to know us and to let us get to know Him. And then He offered Himself as the sacrifice for our sin… His perfect life taking the place of ours, to reconcile us and restore us back to the Father. **Romans 5:8** says,

> **"but God demonstrates His own love toward us, in that**
> **while we were yet sinners, Christ died for us."**

And that was His plan, all along. His life and His death and His resurrection changed everything. Once and for all, and all at once. And to make sure that we grasped the full picture of who He really was, and who we can become in Him, He devised a plan, that each of us would get to know Him in a personal way. When He was walking the earth, and doing ministry, He called twelve disciples to follow Him. Many more followed His teaching of course, but He chose twelve to walk with Him, to know Him, to learn His ways, so they could carry on His gospel. Here is what Jesus has to say to the disciples in the closing words of the gospel of Matthew…

> **Matthew 28:18-20.**
> **18 "I have been given all authority in heaven and earth. 19**
> ***Therefore go and make disciples* in all the nations, baptiz-**
> **ing them into the name of the Father and of the Son and of**
> **the Holy Spirit, 20 and then teach these new disciples to obey**
> **all the commands I have given you; and be sure of this—**
> **that *I am with you always,* even to the end of the world."**

So, we see in the command, known as "the Great Commission," that of course, as believers, there is a call to go and tell the good news of the gospel of Jesus Christ. The words of Jesus to "go and tell," were poured into the foundation of His parting words to us, and instrumental in the spread of the gospel.

But let's not miss the other crucial words that were also poured into that foundation. *In His very last sentence to us, Jesus says, "I am with you always."*

He was leaving, and yet, His words were, "I will be with you."

So, ultimately, we can walk out the words of Jesus, knowing it is a "both/and" kind of command. It really is both, "go and tell," *and* "go and tell no one." As followers of Jesus and modern-day disciples walking the earth today, His words speak as instructions to us, as well. We are to go and tell, making disciples in all the nations, teaching the gospel of Jesus.

And…. as followers of Jesus, we can also Remember and Rest, as we abide in the Secret and the Sacred with Him. We can remember that He is always with us, that our Sacred moments alone with Him, that no one else ever even needs to know about, are the real treasure. We can recall to our hearts and minds, that He promised us, "My presence will go withyou, and I will give you rest." We can carry deep in our hearts, the truth we find in the "go and tell no one" passages, knowing that Jesus Himself, treasures those moments in the Secret and the Sacred.

Acts, chapter 4 gives an amazing account of the way the disciples went on to live out their faith and follow in obedience to carry the gospel of Jesus to the world, just as He'd said. The words in Acts 4:13-14 paint a beautiful picture of what a life lived *with Jesus* can look like.

Acts 4:13 (NLT)
13 The members of the council were amazed when they saw the boldness of Peter and John, for they could see that they were ordinary men with no special training in the Scriptures. They also recognized them as men who had been with Jesus.

May that be true of us….

As we "go and tell," may it be from the "go and tell no one" posture,
of *having been with Jesus.*

Today, as I Remember and Rest in the Secret and the Sacred, this is my prayer…

Day 6/ Remember

Lord, would You bring to my remembrance all that You've taught me from Your Word these last few weeks.

Jesus, when I think about Your words in the "go and tell no one" encounters that we read about in the gospels, I remember...

Jesus, when I think about the way that You so often, drew people into a secret and sacred encounter, away from the eyes of the crowd, I remember...

When I think about the gospel passages we read, and about the countless people who came to You, with an inadequate picture of who You are, and what You could really bring to their lives, I remember...

Jesus, when I think about Your Sermon on the Mount, in Matthew 5 and 6, and Your words that guarded against a life of faith, lived out in public with a desire to be seen or noticed or even applauded, I remember…

When I think about Mary, and how she "pondered these things and treasured them in her heart," I am reminded again, Lord that *You* are the true treasure, and all the richest treasures of wisdom and knowledge are in the mystery of the Secret Place withyou. When I think about the Secret and the Sacred, I remember…

When I think about the disciples that were carrying the gospel and living out the Great Commission, I remember how they were described in that beautiful passage in Acts 4:13. I remember how it was noted that they *"were ordinary men with no special training in the Scriptures,"* but people could recognize them as *"men who had been with Jesus."* Lord, may that be true of me today. Even if I've had no special training, and even if I feel ordinary, will You bring to my remembrance that the same was said of the disciples, *whom Jesus chose*, and that it was their time in the presence of Jesus and their relationship *with Him* that made them winsome image-bearers of Christ and His gospel. Holy Spirit, bring to my remembrance, that it is the *"with-ness"* of Jesus that has set me apart, and equipped me for good works planned in advance for me. Nothing I have ever done, or could ever do makes me worthy to walk as Your disciple…it is in what *You have already done Jesus*, and what I find in the Secret and Sacred withyou Jesus, where I find my purpose, my significance, my calling, my worth, and my rest.
That is the prayer of my heart today…would you help me to walk in it?

When I continue to dwell in the Secret Place of the Most High, and I rest in Your shadow, God Almighty, I remember…

Today, Lord, I want to Remember and Rest in the Secret and the Sacred, and this is the prayer of my heart…

Hallelujah! You who serve God, praise God!
Just to speak His name is praise!
Just to *remember* God is a blessing—
Now and tomorrow and always.
From east to west, from dawn to dusk,
keep lifting all your praises to God!
Psalm 113:1-3

Day 7/ Rest

Lord, I am so grateful for the truth and promises of Your Word. I delight in Your Words, and I continue to seek understanding as I follow You, all the days of my life. May Your Words take root in my heart. Your Words are a lamp unto my feet, and a light unto my path. May I allow them to lead me in the way, everlasting.

By giving me Your Word, You have given me new eyes to see, and opened my heart to true rest, that comes with being in Your Presence.

I remember Your Word that says, "My Presence will go withyou, and I will give you rest." I can value, celebrate and treasure those Secret and Sacred moments withyou, knowing, that you are the treasure and that withyou, I find rest.

When the world or my circumstances tempt me to forget, I will remember the gracious and kind way you invite me into the Secret and Sacred, withyou. Lord, I remember again that abiding in you, is on ongoing continuous, action. Today, I position myself to abide in you, no matter what my circumstances are. Lord, this is the confession of my heart…

Lord, today I come before you with open hands in surrender. If you have "*go and tell*" moments for me today, may I enter into those moments from the place of having been withyou, Jesus. And if today holds "*go and tell no one*" moments for me, Lord help me to Remember and Rest in the Secret and Sacred intimacy I have withyou, there.

Jesus, in light of all that I've studied and learned from your Word in these last weeks, and as I position my heart to Remember and Rest in the Secret and the Sacred withyou, even if I choose to go and tell no one, but you Jesus, this is my prayer....

Matthew 11:28-30 (MSG)
28-30 "Are you tired? Worn out? Burned out on religion? Come to me. Get away with me and you'll recover your life. I'll show you how to take a real rest. Walk with me and work with me—watch how I do it. Learn the unforced rhythms of grace. I won't lay anything heavy or ill-fitting on you. Keep company with me and you'll learn to live freely and lightly."

Appendix: Bible Study Methods

Bible Study Methods

✱ Use this Appendix as you would use a cookbook! There are several resources listed here, to help encourage you and equip you in your own study of God's Word. If you have tools that already work for you, then great... Dive in!

If you would prefer some direction, give this appendix a quick look through. You'll find there are countless resources and tools available. Look at some of the many, different methods out there and see if there is anything that grabs your attention! Try it, make adjustments, additions, or substitutions just like you would if you were adapting a recipe to the tastes of your own family. You know your own learning style, and what may be the best way for you to assimilate God's truth into your life. If after a few days or a week or two, you'd like to try a different method, then go for it! The point is to pray for wisdom, and dive in, trusting the Holy Spirit to make God's real and active word come alive in your heart and transform your life!

A great way to begin, regardless of the method you choose to use for your study is, to begin with, the posture of a teachable heart in *prayer.* (1)

1. Open my eyes to see wonderful things in your Word. {Psalm 119:18}
2. Have mercy on me {Luke 18:38}
3. Make me a doer of your Word. {James 1:22}
4. Open my eyes to Jesus {Luke 24:45}

Different Study Methods

For those that want to keep it very simple and clear, you may want to try:

A. list of questions you ask and answer with each reading:

1. What did this Scripture mean when it was written?
2. What is the timeless truth behind what God is saying?
3. How does it apply to me now?

For those wanting to go a little deeper, you may want to try:

B. Ask and answer the "wh" questions for each chapter:

- Who is talking, and to whom are they speaking?
- What is happening in this text? What happened just before?
- When did this interaction take place? (Answer both, in chronological terms, as well as in the context of what was happening in the life and ministry of Jesus. You can look at what was happening in the passages and chapters before this one, if that helps.)
- Why is this interaction important?
- Where did this happen, and was the location important? Were other people in this same place and able to hear this conversation?
- How does this interaction apply to me?

C. The Precept Observation/Interpretation/Application approach:

1. Observation: What does the text say?
2. Interpretation: What does the text mean?
3. Application: How does it work?

Visit http://www.precept.org/know-gods-word/ (2) for more information

D. Rick Warren's Devotional Method (3):

- Pray for Insight
- Picture It: Visualize the scene in your mind.
- Pronounce it: Say the verse aloud, each time emphasizing a different word.
- Paraphrase it: Rewrite the verse in your own words.
- Personalize it: Replace the pronouns or people in the verse with your own name.
- Pray it: Turn the verse into a prayer and say it back to God.
- Probe it: Ask these 9 questions:

1. Is there a **S**in to confess?
2. Is there a **P**romise to claim? (Have I lacked belief or believed a lie?)
3. Is there an **A**ttitude to change? (do I need to unlearn something or do some hard work?)
4. Is there a **C**ommand to obey?
5. Is there an **E**xample to follow? (or learn from?)
6. Is there a **P**rayer to Pray?
7. Is there an **E**rror to avoid?
8. Is there a **T**ruth to believe?
9. Is there **S**omething for which to praise God?

E. The S.O.A.P. Method: S.O.A.P. stands for Scripture, Observation, Application, and Prayer. Underline or make note of any verses that jump out at you with special significance, record your impressions using the acronym: S.O.A.P.

S: Scripture/ Write the verse or verses that stuck out to you in your reading.
O: Observation/ What did you observe about the scripture that struck you? This can be one sentence or a longer observation.
A: Application/ How can you apply the observation so that it affects your life today?
P: Prayer/ Write out a prayer to God based on what you just learned and ask him to help you apply this truth in your life.

F. Ask, Answer, Accumulate, Apply (4)

1. Ask key questions to provide insight into the meaning of the text. (WH questions, are there key words, comparisons/contrasts, repetitions, progressions, tense, structure?)
2. Answer the questions using the text, and additional tools
3. Accumulate practical principles: Is there: sin to forsake, promises to claim, examples to follow, commands to obey, summary thought?
4. Apply these Biblical truths to your life and relationships: with God, yourself, spouse, family, others

G. Read, Reflect, Record, Respond (5)

Read

1. Read aloud. This is especially helpful in devotional literature like the Psalms.
2. Read carefully. Don't be mechanical; try to be alert and observant.
3. Read repeatedly. Additional readings will give you greater insight into a passage.
4. Read peripherally. As you read a text, think about its context.

Reflect

1. Reflect purposefully. As you reflect upon the passage you are reading or have just completed, do it with the clear purpose of knowing God better and becoming more conformed to the image of His Son.
2. Reflect imaginatively. Actively use your mind's eye to visualize the situation and put yourself in it.
3. Reflect humbly. Never take the Bible for granted; remember that you are privileged to reflect upon the revelation of the living God.
4. Reflect prayerfully. Personalize your reading by communicating with God about the truth you derive from it.
5. Reflect patiently. Reflection takes time and concentration. Include this in the time you have allotted for your reading.

Record

When an important verse, thought, or application emerges from the text, jot it down so that you can retain it and refer to it in the future.

Respond

1. Respond with a confession. When the Word exposes an area of sin in your attitudes or actions, quickly respond by acknowledging it so that you will continue to walk in the light.
2. Respond with faith. Stand upon the truth of what you are reading.
3. Respond with obedience. Resolve to take the truth you have just seen and put it into practice during the remainder of the day.

Using Different Bible Translations

It can be helpful to incorporate the study of several different Bible translations when reading a passage. Our English translations of the Old Testament are translated from Hebrew, and our translations of the New Testament are translated from Greek. The different translations occur because sometimes there are simply not exact, precise English equivalents to the words used in the original language. With so many different Bible translations, it may help to understand the basic differences between each. Word-for-word (also known as formal equivalence) translations attempt to match the original language words with the closest English language counterpart. Thought-for-thought (also known as dynamic equivalence) translations attempt to pair the ideas behind each phrase or sentence with a similar idea in the English language. For more information about each type of Bible translation, see these resources:

http://www.mardel.com/bibleTranslationGuide

http://bibleresources.americanbible.org/resource/a-brief-description-of-popular-bible-translations

https://bible.org/article/why-so-many-versions

Some helpful sources and links for personal study and research:

After engaging in your own personal study, consider consulting some of these helpful resources for a deeper study of the text. They include trusted commentaries, background information resources, dictionaries, and websites that can be helpful when looking up the context of a passage, comparing translations, or researching single words in the original language.

Resources:
Key Word Study Bible
Strong's Exhaustive Concordance of the Bible
Vine's Complete Expository Dictionary of the Old and New Testaments
Bible Dictionary or Bible Encyclopedia
Comparative Study Bible
Word Studies
Interlinear Bible

Links for Helpful Study Tools Online:

https://www.biblegateway.com/

http://www.biblestudytools.com/

http://www.biblestudytools.com/interlinear-bible/

https://www.blueletterbible.org

http://www.biblestudytools.com/concordances/strongs-exhaustive-concordance/

http://www.biblestudytools.com/dictionaries/

http://studybible.info/

http://biblehub.com/

https://bible.org

http://www.biblestudytools.com/commentaries/

EndNotes

Introduction
1. 2 Timothy 3:16 (ESV), Hebrews 4:12-13 (ESV)

Week 1
1. "The Daily Study Bible, Revised Edition, The Gospel of Matthew, Volume 1" by William Barclay, p. 341, 349

2. http://www.ligonier.org/learn/devotionals/messianic-secret/

Week 2
1. Eugene Peterson, Eat This Book: A Conversation in the Art of Spiritual Reading (Grand Rapids: Eerdmans, 2006), p. 55, 57.

2. hub.com pulpit commentary

3. https://www.theatlantic.com/health/archive/2014/08/littering-and-following-the-crowd/374913/

Week 3

1. http://biblehub.com/greek/2323.htm

2. http://biblehub.com/greek/2390.htm

3. http://biblehub.com/greek/4982.htm

Week 4
1. https://www.compellingtruth.org/alms.html

2. http://biblehub.com/greek/2300.htm

3. https://www.blueletterbible.org/Comm/guzik_david/StudyGuide_Mat/Mat_6.cfm

4. http://biblehub.com/greek/5009.htm

5. http://biblehub.com/hebrew/6090.htm

6. http://biblehub.com/greek/991.htm

Week 5

1. "reward": http://biblehub.com/greek/3408.htm

2. "they might be honored by men": http://biblehub.com/greek/1392.htm

3. "will reward": http://biblehub.com/greek/591.htm

4. "treasure": http://biblehub.com/greek/2344.htm

5. Mary "treasured up these things": http://biblehub.com/greek/4933.htm

6. "pondered": http://biblehub.com/greek/4820.htm

Week 6

1. Psalm 91:1: http://biblehub.com/hebrew/5643.htm

2. http://biblehub.com/hebrew/5117.htm

3. http://biblehub.com/hebrew/3427.htm

4. http://biblehub.com/hebrew/3885.htm

Appendix: Bible Study Methods

1. http://www.desiringgod.org/articles/four-prayers-for-bible-reading

2. Precept Ministries International, http://www.precept.org/know-gods-word/

3. http://pastorrick.com/devotional/english/spacepets-probe-the-bible-with-these-questions

4. https://bible.org/seriespage/vi-studying-bible

5. https://bible.org/seriespage/vi-studying-bible as taken from "Enjoy Your Bible" Irving L. Jensen

Photography:

Cover Photography by Aaron Burden

Interior images in the order they appear, are by the following photographers:

1. Elena Ferrer
2. Felix Russell

3. Emanuel Hahn
4. Andrea Natali
5. Jez Timms
6. Mario Ho
7. Ivana Catina
8. Mark Tegetho
9. Aaron Burden
10. Nathan Lindahl

Meet the Author

Kristin Hill, of Withyou Ministries, is a writer, communicator, and Bible teacher. Kristin is passionate about studying God's Word, and the transformational power it has to bring truth and freedom into the lives of women, through individual and small group Bible Study. Kristin and her husband, Eric, founded Withyou Ministries after almost two decades of ministry in the local church, to students, their families, and men and women. Their heartbeat and mission are to provide resources and experiences to help you rest and remember that God is withyou.

Kristin and Eric live in Milton, Georgia, and together they have three beautiful daughters.

To learn more or connect with Kristin, visit www.withyouministries.com.

47866968R00089

Made in the USA
Columbia, SC
04 January 2019